THE CONQUEST OF AMERICA

By the same author
(until 1972, writing under the name Hans Koningsberger)

FICTION

The Affair, 1958
An American Romance, 1960
A Walk with Love and Death, 1961
I Know What I'm Doing, 1964
The Revolutionary, 1967
Death of a Schoolboy, 1974
The Petersburg-Cannes Express, 1976
The Kleber Flight, 1981
DeWitt's War, 1983
America Made Me, 1983
Acts of Faith, 1988
To the North Pole, forthcoming

NONFICTION

Love and Hate in China (a travel book), 1966
Along the Roads of Russia (a travel book), 1968
The Future of Che Guevara (a biography), 1971
The Almost World (an autobiography), 1971
Columbus: His Enterprise (a biography), 1976, 1991
A New Yorker in Egypt (a travel book), 1976
Nineteen Sixty-Eight, a Personal Report (report of a year),
  1987
The Conquest of America (a history), 1993

THE CONQUEST OF AMERICA

How the Indian Nations Lost Their Continent

HANS KONING

**MONTHLY REVIEW PRESS
NEW YORK**

Library of Congress Cataloging-in-Publication Data
Koning, Hans, 1921-
 The conquest of America / by Hans Koning.
  p. cm. — (Cornerstone Books)
 Includes bibliographical references.
 ISBN 0-85345-877-4 : $22.00. — ISBN 0-85345-876-6 (pbk.) : $10.00
 1. America—History. 2. Indians—Wars. 3. Indians—Government relations.
4. America—Discovery and exploration. I. Title. II. Series: Cornerstone books
(New York, N.Y.)
E18.K79 1993
970.01—dc20   93-24482
                                                       CIP

Monthly Review Press
122 West 27th Street
New York, NY 10001

Manufactured in the United States of America
10 9 8 7 6 5 4 3 2 1

To Tess, Chris, and Andrew,
and all children in a happier world

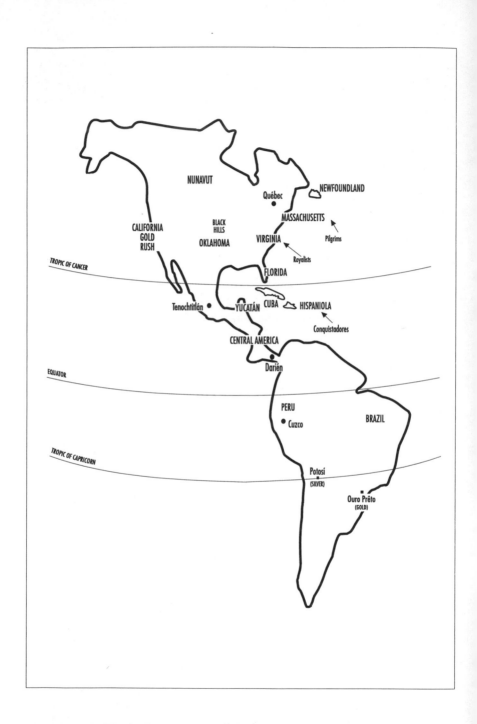

CONTENTS

ABOUT THIS BOOK

We all know by now that the European presence in the Americas has passed the five-hundred-year mark. The landfall of Columbus in the West Indies was in October 1492, and in the year 1992 it was commemorated, or mourned. There were still people who celebrated it, but I think they were terribly wrong. I have told why in my book *Columbus: His Enterprise.* What you have here is the sequel, which carries that story forward to the present day.

Ever since Columbus' fateful landing, Europeans, members of the "white race," have lived on the American continent. I put "white race" between quotes because "race" is no longer accepted as a proper scientific term. That is not to say that people don't think they know exactly what they mean when they talk of the white race, or the black race. The reality of races and racism is with us every day.

Over the past five centuries, the whites have taken away this continent, all of it, from the Indian nations. The Spaniards who colonized most of what is now Latin America talked of their actions as the *Conquista*, the Conquest, which is precisely what it was. Up north the tendency is toward euphemisms and of how the West was "won," leaving out whom it was won (that is, taken) from. It was of course a conquest too.

This book documents the history of both those conquests and how they turned America from an Indian continent into a white-ruled one. It is not a pretty story, but bear in mind that I am presenting hard facts, not theories or opinions. If we do not learn from our history, we are doomed to repeat it. It is time for us all to look at our past with critical eyes. A country able to do just that has a very fine reason to be proud of itself, a better reason for pride than the past deeds of a false hero.

I am thinking of course of Columbus. I call him a false hero because at some point in the nineteenth century, and mainly here in the United States, he was falsely turned into a kind of founder-hero for the New World, a symbol of white civilization bringing light to a dark continent. That is the way he used to be presented to our children and it was not an innocent presentation: it was a myth that made them look at themselves and at this country in the false light of white arrogance and of racism. Most of the account and most of its details were fantasy, but what was left out, and why, was even more important than the mistakes and fantasies that were left in. All this was the reason for writing *Columbus: His Enterprise.* Columbus deserved a book of his own because we have to deal with this Columbus legacy.

I know it was not easy for many people to do that. The story of the blue-eyed hero of their grade-school days was dear to them. But Columbus was only the beginning. The trail of the bloody conquest he set into motion leads on, right into our time. And if we continue to close our eyes to it, we will not overcome it.

Those of you who had trouble with *Columbus: His Enterprise* will have even more trouble with this sequel.

But I am dealing in facts; please give them a chance.

1

THE CONQUEST OF AMERICA

The Europeans who came to the Americas, either to get rich and then go home or to settle here for a new life, haven't been gracious visitors. They took over the land at all possible speed. In the process, they enslaved or killed most of the original Americans.

It is a testimony to the amazing tenacity of the human spirit amidst disaster that millions of native Americans—Indians, as we have come to call them—are surviving as Indians today. In the United States their number, from an all-time low of perhaps 300,000 around the year 1900, has risen again to 2 million.

THOSE WHO WERE HERE BEFORE

Historians used to tell us that maybe 10 million people were living in all of the Americas before the year 1492. In what is now the United States and Canada, a million hunters and nomads were supposed to have roamed the plains and forests. Until about fifty years ago, this was the generally accepted wisdom.

We now know that this estimate was totally mistaken. Anthropologists, agrarian sociologists, and many other scholars have gone over the continent acre by acre, back through history. They measured the farmland and calculated how many people it could have fed. They studied ruins of Indian towns, irrigation canals, graveyards, tax documents from the 1400s. The longer they worked, the larger the population figures became. Now we have a figure of 10 million people just for Canada and the United States. For Mexico, the estimate is now 20 to 30 million people. And the total figure for Latin America ranges from a low of 65 million to a high of more than 100 million—both figures higher than the entire population of Europe at the time. We also know that the first inhabitants of the Americas came from Asia thousands of years earlier than scholars once believed. Of course, the fewer Indians had lived here and the shorter the time they had been here, the easier it had been to see the Conquest as just one more wave in the ebb and flow of populations throughout history. But this was not an empty wilderness, or a newly settled continent. It was a densely populated land area, with many large towns. How could such a place have been "discovered" by Europeans?

NORTH AND SOUTH OF THE BORDER

When writing of the Americas, I use modern geographical names. It would be too hard on the reader to do otherwise. But we must be aware of the fact that the continent's streams, mountains, and lakes had been named before any white person had seen them. The poet who described Daniel Boone "as bestowing names on streams and founts, on plants and places yet anonymous" (the year was 1813) was painting out the Indians, turning them into non-people.

America itself was named after an early sixteenth century Italian traveler named Amerigo Vespucci. No Indian living here had an image of the whole hemisphere, so it had no name; and therefore you could argue that this was a legitimate naming. We can call ourselves lucky: compared with the *conquistadores* (the Spanish invaders and conquerors), Amerigo was an enlightened man, and one of the first scientific navigators.

The tradewinds that blow across the Atlantic Ocean follow a steady pattern. Summer and winter, one set of winds blows steadily from the northeast, starting at the Tropic of Cancer, a circle around the earth at 23 1/2° northern latitude, and dying out near the equator. North of the Tropic, another set of winds blows from the American coast to Europe, where they bend south. (Latitude is the distance in degrees to the equator. From the north or south pole to the equator is 90°.)

The east and west winds form a flattened circle. The east winds blew Christopher Columbus, Amerigo Vespucci, and all who came after them from Spain and Portugal to the West Indies. The westerlies blew them home. But that same circle of winds kept the first English, French and Dutch ships away from the West Indies. Once they knew there was land out there, they got to the North American coast, but much farther north and with much greater effort, tacking up against the west winds. This pattern of invisible air currents had a dramatic effect on the fates of these two parts of the continent, north and south.

The circle of latitude that runs through the city of Dallas, Texas (32 1/2° north), more or less follows the great divide created by the ocean winds. Below that line, America was invaded and conquered by the Spaniards (except for Brazil, which fell to the Portuguese.) In the early years those invaders were mostly soldiers of fortune, assorted penniless *hidalgos* (self-styled gentlemen, too proud to do manual work), and a few priests. Their main idea was to collect gold and take it back home. Above the dividing line, the Conquest was largely the work of colonizers from Britain, Ireland, and northern Europe, men and women

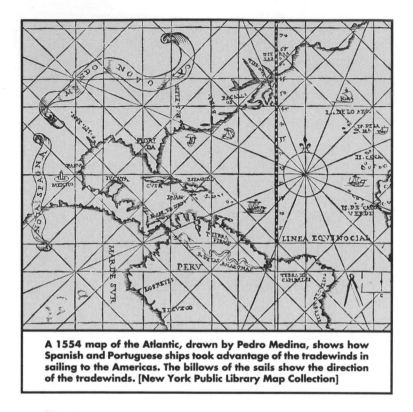

A 1554 map of the Atlantic, drawn by Pedro Medina, shows how Spanish and Portuguese ships took advantage of the tradewinds in sailing to the Americas. The billows of the sails show the direction of the tradewinds. [New York Public Library Map Collection]

who left their homes for good and who became independent farmers and merchants.

From the beginning the Spaniards saw the native Americans as natural slaves, beasts of burden, part of the loot. When working them to death was more economical than treating them somewhat humanely, they worked them to death. The English, on the other hand, had no use for the native peoples. They saw them as devil worshippers, savages who were beyond salvation by the church, and exterminating them increasingly became accepted policy.

THE GAP OF AGES

If so many millions of people lived in the Americas before the Europeans arrived, how were they so quickly subjugated by so few invaders? The answer to this question has several parts.

There was, first of all, the fact that the Indian nations, like those of Europe at the time, were often divided among themselves. The Europeans were able to use one tribe or nation as an ally in the fight against another tribe or nation, until it had served its purpose and could in turn be treated as the enemy.

Another strike against the Indians was their lack of resistance to European diseases. It is now generally assumed that this continent was amazingly healthy, probably because domestic animals and cattle were rare or nonexistent. But this made the native Americans deadly vulnerable to European smallpox, tuberculosis, and other diseases. They were swept away by the thousands because they had not built up immunities to these diseases. Smallpox, for instance, played a major role in the final defeat of the Aztecs by Hernando Cortés.

But the root cause of the Indian downfall was the time gap, a gap of thousands of years of technological development which separated the west coast of Europe from the east coast of America. Just as one modern infantry battalion or a couple of tanks would wipe out all of Napoleon's armies, so the Spaniards with their armor and the Englishmen with their muskets could wipe out whole Indian nations without suffering a single casualty. In many regions, American Indian agriculture was ahead of European agriculture. In many regions there was a high civilization of art, architecture, and thought. But nowhere had the technology of war reached even the level of the ancient Assyrians, with their horses, chariots, and bronze or iron knives and swords. The Indians, north or south, had no iron or steel, no armor, no gunpowder, no horses, no attack dogs. They fought back, often for years. But by the merciless laws of physics and the science of war, they had to lose in the end.

A RECKONING

I cannot help but hesitate a moment before opening the bloody record of the Conquest. You have to be careful, writing about history. Humanity has a long and cruel past, and I would not soon label something done on this earth as "without precedent." But we have to live with the fact that most nations and most men (and, more rarely, women) have under certain historical circumstances been capable of terrible deeds. It is our duty to try and understand how such things could happen and, indeed, still happen and how they can be stopped. Indeed, in our days, for the first time, people are beginning to see themselves as their brothers' and sisters' keepers, across all borders. There is still hope for the likes of us.

2

THE EARLY SPANISH MAIN

The Age of Exploration, of the first great sea voyages by Europeans, did not start by chance. When the Turks captured Constantinople (now called Istanbul) in 1543, they closed the land route from Europe to the Orient. That put an end to the only important international trade of the time: trade in silks, spices, gold, and other luxuries that came by caravan from Central Asia, India, and the Far East to the eastern end of the Mediterranean. The fall of Constantinople also led to an exodus of Greek scholars, who fled to the West, where they gave learning and science a new impetus.

Those were the closing years of the Middle Ages. People were no longer content to view life as a closed circle, a pilgrimage under the watchful eye of the Church. Change stopped being a bad word; individualism became the new creed. Ambitious men decided to outflank the Turks and trade with the Orient by sea. At the same time, improvements in ship design and developments in the science of astronomy made sea voyages less risky. Spain and Portugal were the most modern nations; France and England were still more deeply medieval.

THE SPAIN OF FERDINAND AND ISABELLA

Spain, which had once consisted of many small kingdoms, was unified through the marriage of Ferdinand, King of Aragon, and Isabella, Queen of Castille, who jointly ruled the entire country after 1479. The only exception was the Moorish kingdom of Granada, which surrendered to the Spanish armies on January 2, 1492. From that point on, the two monarchs set to work creating an absolute kingdom. They made racial purity—*limpieza de sangre*—the most important qualification for citizenship. Within months, a royal decree expelled all Spanish Jews. It was soon followed by one expelling all Muslims (contrary to what the king had promised them at the surrender of Granada). The Roman Catholic church was set to stamp out all heresy. The old nobility, which had lost its independence, still owned the land, and their most tangible wealth were their sheep, 3 million of them. But sheep did enormous damage to the crops, which led to periodic famines among the peasants; at the same time, Spanish wool ran into increasing competition from England and Flanders. Ferdinand and Isabella needed to look for wealth elsewhere to finance the Big Power role they wanted to play. In the same year as the fall of Granada, 1492, they gave the go-ahead to the Genoese sailor and trader named Christopher Columbus, who had been petitioning them for years with his plan to reach the Orient by sailing westward. They had little to lose: the whole expedition was to cost, in pre-1914 gold dollars, $7,000. And they had much to gain.

Portugal was already trying to find a sea route to the Orient, and it was rumored to be close to success. It had established trading stations along the west coast of Africa, and it would not be long before a Portuguese—aided by a black pilot from East

Africa—reached India. But the Pope had granted Portugal sole rights to the Africa route, which meant that Spain had to go west, as Columbus proposed.

THE CASE OF COLUMBUS

I will only sum up briefly what my book *Columbus: His Enterprise* deals with at length.

Without doubt Christopher Columbus was a sailor with a natural feeling for winds and currents; he was also a very lucky one. His astronomical observations, as noted in his logs, were hopelessly wrong, but he may well have known better and written them down incorrectly so that he could keep his true whereabouts a secret from his crew and his competitors.

Columbus was not the only man who knew that the world was round—no educated person in his day thought the world was flat. The problem with his plan was that there was no ship that could carry supplies all the way from the west coast of Portugal to the east coast of China or Japan, as he meant to do. The world was much larger than Columbus believed: such a voyage would have been 12,000 miles rather than the 3,000 he planned. He and his crew would have died if they hadn't been saved by the fact that they reached land after traveling 3,000 miles—only that land was America, not Asia. Nevertheless, to his dying day he insisted that it was Asia that he had reached.

No one can take Columbus' achievement as a sailor away from him: his landfall in the West Indies in 1492 is one of history's big "firsts." If he had not reached the Americas, some other European would have been first—probably the Portuguese captain who landed in 1500, per chance, in what is now Brazil. (The history of this continent would not have been much different: the Portuguese in Brazil behaved just like the Spaniards elsewhere.) Such "ifs" do not diminish Columbus' initiative. But Columbus and his companions were not the "founders" of America, or even the "first immigrants," as some books have called them. They hated the lands they had discovered; they wanted only to loot them and go home. Columbus was the man "who started the bloody trail of the Conquest," to quote Bartolomé de las Casas, the Dominican friar who arrived in America before 1500 and who became the chronicler of those early years. Whatever he did as a sailor is darkly overshadowed by what he did on land, and in the end he will be judged by his deeds ashore.

For seven years, from 1493 until 1500, he was governor of the island he had called Espaniola or Hispaniola (which is now divided between Haiti and the Dominican Republic). After his first landfall in October 1492, he had written to the Court in Madrid, "Hispaniola is a miracle ... both fertile and beautiful. The inhabitants are so tractable, so peaceable, astonishingly shy.... They are so free with their possessions, when you ask for something they never say no. To the contrary, they offer to share with anyone. They are of great intelligence." But he ended, "If your Majesties so wish, all can be carried to Spain or made slaves on their island." This was the first and last time that Columbus would wrote admiringly of the local people, the Arawaks (or Tainos, as other writers call them). From then on, they were "savages."

Columbus had promised mountains of gold to his king and queen, and his obsessive need to fulfill this promise led to the death of half the population during his rule. At least half a million people died, perhaps more. The Indians were sent to collect gold from the streams and to bring it to the Spanish fort. Those who met their quota—a tiny bell full of gold dust every three months—were given a kind of dog tag to hang around their necks. Those who were found without such a tag had their hands cut off. Those who fled into the mountains were hunted with dogs. The chiefs, or *caciques*, were burned alive to quench any taste for rebellion; they were hanged in rows of thirteen above fires of green wood. (Why thirteen? That was "in honor of our Redeemer and His twelve apostles," as de las Casas tells us.)

It was considered good military policy by the Spanish *conquista-dores* to give their dogs a "taste for Indian flesh." An engraving by the Flemish artist Theodore de Bry used in Bartolomé de las Casas's *The Devastation of the Indies.* [New York Public Library Rare Books and Manuscripts Collection]

When no more gold could be found, Columbus turned to the slave trade. In 1498 he wrote that 4,000 slaves a year could be shipped to Spain "at a clear profit of 20 million *marevedis*" (about $400,000 in pre-1914 dollars). That way, he said, he could still deliver the profits he had promised. But the slaves died too quickly, and when this scheme too had run its course, Columbus divided the land and the remaining Indians among his followers. Each could run his *encomienda,* his estate, as he saw fit, or he could sell (or rent out) the Indians on it as slaves to work in the mines in other parts of "New Spain." The heritage of this system, large estates worked by landless peasants, still weighs down on Latin America, where in many countries the "few own the many."

During the seven years Columbus was governor, the native population of the island committed mass suicide. Men and women ate poisoned roots. Women killed their newborn babies. Epidemics swept across the island, while the birth rate dropped to near zero. (In "natural" epidemics, such as Europe's plagues of the time, the birth rate shoots up immediately afterward.) The Arawaks, who had once believed that the white men from the east were gods, now called them *yares,* or demons. When Nicolas de Ovando, a successor of Columbus on Hispaniola, was met on his arrival by the eighty-four caciques who were still alive, they begged for peace. He had them burned alive in the house where they were meeting—except for their queen, Anacoana, whom he had hanged. Ten years after Columbus' death, the Dominican priest Pedro de Cordóba wrote to the king: "People so gentle, obedient, and good have been kept at excessive labors so that in Hispaniola alone more than a million of your subjects have been destroyed." And during the entire period Columbus was governor of the island, not one native American was converted to the Catholic faith.

HOW DO WE KNOW?

How can we know all this? The Spanish empire-to-be quickly became the most bureaucratic and best documented territory ever known. Not a month went by without some inspector arriving to check on everything—if only to make sure the king was receiving his share of the loot. The archives in Seville house millions of reports and documents on the Conquest. And everything Bartolomé de las Casas wrote about the Conquest is confirmed there.

De las Casas was a friend of Columbus and came to America as a friar; he would be the first ordained bishop in the hemisphere.

He himself owned slaves, but in 1514 he suddenly saw what was happening to the Indians. He would spend the rest of his long life trying to save them. He wrote a book entitled *A Very Short Report on the Destruction of the Indies,* and he put the words "very short" *(brevissima)* in the title in hopes of increasing the chance that the king would read it. For some years, when he was bishop of what is now Mexico, de las Casas refused to give absolution to dying Spanish *conquistadores* unless they freed their slaves and returned their loot; the Church ordered him to end this practice.

Here is how de las Casas described the famous landfall: "Into this sheepfold, this land of meek outcasts" (he calls the Indians on Hispaniola "outcasts" because they weren't Christians) "came some Spaniards who immediately behaved like ravening and wild beasts ... with the strangest and most varied methods of cruelty, never seen or heard of before." He ends: "I have not described a thousandth part of what the Indians endured. God is my witness."

AFTER COLUMBUS

The Spanish Main was the half-circle of islands from Cuba and Hispaniola in the west around to Trinidad in the southeast, including the nearby coasts of South America and Central America. "Spanish Main" used to have a romantic ring to it. It made you think of buccaneers and sword fights, scoundrels redeemed by their chivalry. But there was nothing chivalrous about the way it was conquered.

These were the first territories that the *conquistadores* took for Spain. The entire military operation was completed by about 1515, and by 1550 all the gold to be found had been collected and shipped back to Spain and the original population had been exterminated. The once blessed islands had been turned into "deserts," as we can read in the official reports written by Friar Motolinia, Pedro Cieza de León, Alfonso de Zurito, Fernández de Oviedo, and dozens of others.

"Spaniards lance Indian men, women, and children they meet on the road, from their horses, at the slightest provocation or indeed without any provocation," wrote one local governor. There was a *rage* to the cruelty and destruction for which the word "racism" is ridiculously weak. It was as if these men had been waiting all their lives to do this. If it would make sense in some nightmarishly amoral world to kill all the *caciques* and leave the Indians without leaders, it still remains incomprehensible why they were tortured to death on slow fires of green wood. It remains incomprehensible why these "shy and peaceable" men and women were not only worked to death in mines and on plantations but were killed for sport whenever a Spaniard felt like it. As de las Casas wrote, the Indians "were not treated like cattle but like the excrement of cattle in the public square."

I think now that, contrary to what one might expect and contrary to the Spaniards' professed religion, it was their meekness that enraged the *conquistadores*. Their inwardness and their humility made them, literally, God-given victims in the eyes of their conquerors.

DEATH OF THE ISLANDS

At first most of the loot came from Hispaniola. After that, Puerto Rico and Cuba headed the list. Every grain of gold, and later of silver, had to go to Spain—a Spaniard selling gold elsewhere could receive the death penalty. In Spain the gold was weighed, registered by the clerks in the Casa de la Contratación in Seville, and locked in the famous Green Chest. Three keys were needed to open the chest; each was held by a different government official.

We know "everything": we know that between 1503 and 1510, 4,965 kilos and 180 grams of gold were shipped from the islands to Seville. We may find justice in the fact that all that gold and silver did not help Spain. Prices and wages doubled and tripled. Inflation destroyed the living of a large part of the peasantry. The wars that the kings waged in Europe with their gold were all lost. By the late eighteenth century, Spain had become one of the poorest and most backward nations in Europe.

When new gold was found on Hispaniola in "placers"—gravel deposits containing gold that had been eroded from its original bedrock—the Spaniards sailed to Florida and Curaçao to find slaves to mine it. The Bahamas, which they had called "useless islands" because they held no gold, now had their entire population kidnapped and taken to Hispaniola to work in the new mines. They all died, 40,000 of them. Thus in 1513 the Bahamas had become "the first wholly depopulated part of the New World." The document that reported this operation says that the Spanish slavers were taking the Bahama (Lucaya) Indians to Hispaniola "to be instructed in the Catholic faith."

Columbus' original grant of perpetual governorship of the islands (for him *and* his descendants) was never cancelled, but by then it had long been ignored. Yet until his death King Ferdinand granted him one-tenth of the royal fifth, that is to say, 2 percent of all the loot, and thus Columbus died—contrary to myth—a very rich man.

Now Ferdinand himself appointed and fired governors, and issued licenses for new expeditions. Once the Spanish had mapped the north coast of the South American continent, from the isthmus of Panama to the Brazilian hump, they realized that there was no direct sea route to the Orient and the spices of the (real) Indies. But on the shores of the Gulf of Darién, where Panama and Colombia meet, they met Indians with enormous treasures of gold ornaments. The Indian town of Darién was occupied by the Spaniards in 1510, and, with Darién as their base, they set up slave and treasure hunts all along the Atlantic coastline of Tierra Firme, as they named the continent of South America. The gold was soon looted and on its way to Spain and the center of gravity of the Conquest would move away from the West Indian islands. The Spaniards who remained were impatient to seek their fortunes in new lands.

Fifty years later, according to the official documents, fewer than 1,500 Spaniards lived on all the islands of the Caribbean. Some of these islands had now acquired a new life, not much less horrible than under the gold fever. Enslaved Africans now worked on large sugar plantations. They had become the main population: 12,000 of them were working on Hispaniola. The number of Indians remaining: none.

MEANWHILE, BACK HOME

The people in Spain—those who wanted to know—were well informed of what was happening in the new colonies. You may have read that the king and queen "didn't really know" and that before her death in 1505 Queen Isabella had tried to stop the enslavement of people who were supposedly now subjects of the Crown. But although the Crown issued slave-raiding licenses that specified that the Indians were to be taken "as nearly as possible with their consent," it is hard to find any sense in that phrase. Some years after Isabella's death, King Ferdinand wrote, "Our Lord is well served in the bringing of Indians from the outlying islands to where the gold is" (that is, to places where the original population had been worked to death), "although," the king added, "so many die before getting to the mines that this is somewhat burdensome on the conscience, and not very profitable to the business at hand."

The king may have looked at the enterprise with a practical mind, but the lawyers and priests who hung around the Court and in the university towns of Spain kept an abstract, academic debate about the rights and wrongs of enslavement going for most of the sixteenth century. Were the Indians human beings or some kind of demons or maybe even apes? In other words, did they have souls, no souls, or possibly half a soul each? And if they had souls, did the Spaniards still have the right to enslave them?

As always in that kind of debate, the contestants seemed to have a direct line to God, whose will they quoted with great ease. "Just as Joshua [in the Old Testament] was willed by God to destroy the people of Canaan because they were idolaters, thus God willed Spain to destroy the Indians," was one popular statement. The Greek philosopher Aristotle and the Catholic theologian Thomas Aquinas were also good sources to help prove that slavery was a necessary institution. From there a logical chain of argument led to the "proof" that God had *specifically created* the heathen Indians to be slaves to Christian Europeans. One major event in this talk-fest was a debate that was held in Valladolid, Spain, in 1550: for a whole month Bartolomé de las Casas, lonely advocate for the Indians, debated Juan de Sepúlveda, who argued that the Indians were wild animals and could therefore be freely killed or enslaved. It was clear that most of the learned men present were with de Sepúlveda.

Earlier, when holding court in the town of Burgos, the monarchy had issued a set of laws banning the greatest cruelties. The new colonists in America ignored them, and soon they were officially withdrawn.

THE *REQUERIMIENTO*

The years of debate did lead to one document, called the *Requerimiento,* or "Requirement." Its origin was not concern for the Indians, but concern to make Spain's position legally unassailable. It was drawn up by Spain's master jurist, Palacios Rubios, and after 1516 every Spanish expedition was required to carry a copy (the original is still in Seville).

The *Requerimiento* begins by stating that Christ gave St. Peter the task of governing the world, a task since handed down to the Popes, and that the present Pope had given all the islands and mainland of the Ocean Sea (that is, the Atlantic) to Spain. The *Requerimiento* then calls upon the Indians to acknowledge the Church, the Pope, and the king of Spain, and goes on, "If you do so, His Majesty will greet you with all love ... and leave your wives and children free.... He will not compel you to turn Christian unless you ... wish to be converted to our Holy Catholic Faith. But if you do not, or if you maliciously delay in doing so, by the help of God, I will enter into your lands ... and I will take your wives and children and make slaves of them, and will sell them as such, and will take all your goods and do you all the mischief I can."

Every Spanish captain was required to read this document to any Indians he planned to attack or enslave; he then had to give them time to ponder it. This was the legal basis for the Spanish Conquest. The document became a joke among the *conquistadores* and their followers. It would be read out solemnly, in Spanish, to a village whose inhabitants were asleep—or had just been slain. It would be read out to the trees or to a mountain. It saved no Indian. The Spanish soldiers had many good laughs over it. And the words "I will do you all the mischief I can" came true.

By the 1494 Treaty of Tordesillas, Pope Alexander VI had divided the "heathen world" between Spain and Portugal: the dividing line ran north-south, more or less along the meridian of 53° longitude, which cuts across Brazil. Throughout the Conquest, Spain and Portugal abided by Tordesillas, which is the reason that Brazil is the only Portuguese nation on the South American continent. When other European nations began to cross the ocean, they obviously did not accept the claim, but for centuries afterward Spain used it as the legal basis for its garrotting (choking to death with a cord and stick) of foreign sailors caught in "their" half of the world.

In the summer of 1991, the delegates of the indigenous American nations, at a United Nations meeting in Geneva, asked Pope John Paul II to void that division of the world undertaken by Pope Alexander VI in 1494. They did not receive an answer.

3

WAR ON THE AZTECS AND WAR ON THE INCAS

The ease with which the Spaniards were now sailing to the Americas is striking. Their route led through mild climates and over moderate seas, a trip in our days made by amateur yachtsmen. Not for the Spaniards the huge toll in sickness and death that were common for the tropical Portuguese voyages around Africa, which took six months or more. Imagine the change in their view of the world when a wild and empty ocean, scattered with islands where men without heads, dogs with human bodies, and other monsters had lurked, turned into a calm blue sea bordered by beautiful lands.

A stream of adventurers, out-of-work mercenaries, and penniless aristocrats now set out for this continent, while the Spaniards left the ruined islands of the Caribbean for the South American coast. Remember that these men did not see themselves as settlers. Most of them, if they had two pesos to rub together, disdained manual labor. They came to plunder and then go home with their loot. They could not even bother to feed themselves from the produce of these rich lands. They stole the corn from the Indians, and the cargo lists in the Seville archives show that from 1495 on, dried fish was shipped out to them—dried fish, to a place where the Indians could scoop up fish with their hands and fill their canoes "in a moment." Yet this was the way King Ferdinand wanted it. He and his deputy, Juan de Fonseca, archdeacon of Seville, approved each expedition and its crew. They had the ships loaded not with the tools of normal life but with muskets, cannon, horses and dogs, and iron shackles and collars for the slaves. Gold was their only end.

SIGHTING THE PACIFIC

One of the *conquistadores* who was stuck in the Caribbean was Vasco Nuñez de Balboa. After the slaves on his land in Hispaniola died, he moved to Cuba, and from Cuba he joined an expedition to Darién. There he took his part in the plundering of the coastal regions of South America. In 1513, he and his men were trekking through the mountainous terrain of the Isthmus (now Panama) when they suddenly saw the distant shimmering of sunlight on a blue sea ahead of them, to the south. (The Atlantic was behind them, to the north; the Isthmus runs from east to west.) Balboa, so the account of his expedition tells us, ran ahead down the mountainside. Pulling his sword, he waded into the water, slashed the waves, and cried that he was tasking possession of that sea in the name of the Spanish king.

The men returned to Darién on the Atlantic coast "with a great booty" and sent triumphal messages and presents to the king. In response, Ferdinand sent out ships from Spain to exploit this new sea, and he named Balboa "Adelantado" (or governor) "of the South Sea." This sea is now called the Pacific Ocean.

Balboa did not enjoy his title for long. His expedition had set out without a license from the local governor, and his jealous colleagues managed to have him put in prison for breaking the law. Madrid was far away, time passed, and King Ferdinand died. In 1517 Balboa, the first European to lay eyes on the Pacific Ocean, was beheaded in the public square of the town of Panama. It was perhaps a fitting fate for a man who was famous for his mastiff dog, which he had taught to tear the heads off Indians with its teeth.

The Spanish now occupied a beachhead on the Pacific, and they built ships there that gave them mastery over the west coast of South America. Within a few years, Francisco Pizarro, who had been one of Balboa's men, signed a contract with the Spanish Crown that gave him the right to conquer that coast for Spain.

Meanwhile another *conquistador,* stranded on Cuba and "very deeply in debt although he had received good grants ... of Indians," decided to cross to the mainland and explore the far coast of what is now Mexico. His name was Hernando Cortés and he would be the conqueror of the Aztec empire.

THE DESTRUCTION OF THE AZTECS

Cortés sailed from Havana, which was then on the south coast of Cuba and only a hundred nautical miles from the island of Cozumel, which lies just off the coast of the Yucatán peninsula of Mexico. (Some years later, Havana was moved to the north coast of Cuba, which was healthier and safer from pirates.) He landed on Cozumel on March 4, 1519, with eleven ships and five hundred men. Thirteen of them had muskets and thirty-two carried crossbows. They had four small cannon, some bronze guns, and plenty of gunpowder and cannon balls. One of the men brought his own horse, his own black slave, and his own store of cassava and salted pork; he was called "the richest soldier of the whole fleet." Such a detail, and the fact that of those five hundred men only forty-five had more than a sword or lance, shows the scarcity of their means compared to those of modern warfare. Yet to the Indians, the Spanish weapons were overwhelming.

We know this and much else about Cortés and his expedition—down to the time and place he lost a shoe in the mud—because one of his soldiers, Bernal Díaz, wrote (or, more likely, dictated) a long chronicle of it when he was an old man.

The land Cortés invaded was part of the Aztec empire. The Aztecs ruled out of Tenochtitlán, a city built in the middle of a lake where Mexico City now stands. Its population at the time— 300,000, according to the most recent estimates—made it far larger than the London, Paris, or Madrid of the sixteenth century. The Aztecs had subdued their neighboring nations in a series of wars, and by the time Cortés arrived they had established a vast empire. They had built temples, dams, and irrigation canals, and their corn production was much more efficient than Europe's crops of wheat and rye. They wove cotton and used gold and silver in their decorative art. But they had not discovered iron, and their sharpest weapon was a wooden knife with a cutting edge of hard volcanic glass called obsidian.

They also had no horses and no wheel, and their language had not yet developed an alphabet. Instead, a complex system of woven and painted images and colored threads was used to record events and messages. Their architecture amazed the Spaniards with its beauty. A surplus of food was the rule: it has even been argued that Cortés' conquest was possible because of the abundant food supplies he came upon. On the Yucatán peninsula itself, the Mayans formed the dominant nation, the northern outpost of a civilization that stretched south into Central America. (We are only now beginning to become knowledgeable about the Mayans, who in their heyday formed some fifty nations going back to the ninth century, about their splendid architecture and their astronomy, which gave them a calendar more true to the sun than the European one of that century.)

The Aztecs ruled their empire as a theocracy, under the strict guidance of an anguished religion. I call it "anguished" because the existence of humanity, and indeed of the earth itself, was very far from being taken for granted. It was thought to depend on human obedience to a detailed and tyrannical ritual. Life proceeded in cycles. It was up to the priests to see that it would not be extinguished at the end of any one cycle; at those fateful dates all fires had to be put out and relit from one source. And human sacrifice was the main tool in conciliation of the inimical, or at best neutral, gods.

To be thus sacrificed might once have been an honor (as it was in earliest Greece), but it had since deteriorated into a regular massacre of prisoners-of-war and slaves on the temple steps. Finding such victims had probably become the main reason for the wars the Aztecs fought with the neighboring nations they had conquered: Cortés was invading a state divided against itself and surrounded by many enemies. (No doubt the ritual of human sacrifice had become a cancer in the Aztec state. This has been presented as a justification for Cortés, although obviously he would not have acted differently if there had been no such practice.)

In 1519 the Aztec king was Montezuma, the second of that name. He was a mysterious man, intensely religious and superstitious. We have no groundwork of facts allowing us to understand him, as little as we can understand what motivated an Egyptian pharaoh. We know that in that fateful year rumors could have already reached him of invasions by white bearded men from across the seas, gods or demons. An Aztec myth predicted the return of an exiled god, Quetzalcoatl, who was to arrive from the east and bring in a better age. He was white and perhaps bearded.

All this provided Cortés with an ideal playing field for his courage, his diplomacy, his duplicity, and his total absence of conscience and humanity. Within two years he would destroy Tenochtitlan and the Aztec empire and rename it "New Spain."

The story of those two years is gruesome. Listen to Bartolomé de las Casas: "In New Spain, the climax of injustice and violence and tyranny committed against the Indians has been surpassed.

Because the Spaniards have now lost all fear of God and of the king, they have ceased to know right from wrong. They have killed young and old, men, women, and children, some 4 million souls."

As Cortés marched inland from Cozumel down the Yucatán, he soon learned of the fabled capital Tenochtitlán and its king. Local tribes presented themselves as allies and started accompanying him on his march, and Cortés kept his men in order by announcing that any plunderer would be hanged on the spot. Messengers from Montezuma arrived. They carried gold and jewels and his request to the Spaniards that they turn around. Of course the gifts only whetted the Spaniards' appetite for more.

When Cortés had reached the town of Cholula, only sixty miles from Tenochtitlán, Montezuma sent a message begging him to wait. He would himself come out to meet him. De las Casas again: "The Spaniards now agreed to carry out a massacre, or as they called it, a punitive attack in order to sow terror. That was always the determination of the Spaniards in all the lands they conquered. With this aim, they sent a summons to all the *caciques* and nobles ... and as soon as these arrived, they were taken prisoner so unexpectedly that none could flee and warn the others. The Spaniards had asked for five thousand Indians to carry their cargo. What a grievous thing it was, to see those Indians as they prepared to carry the loads. They came naked, stark naked except for their private parts, which they covered. And they had a netting bag slung over their shoulders, holding their meager nourishment. They were all made to squat down on their haunches like tame sheep.

"When they were all placed close together, they were bound and tied. Then at a command, all the Spaniards drew their swords or pikes and while their *caciques* looked on helplessly, all those tame sheep were butchered, cut to pieces. At the end of two days, some survivors came out from under the corpses, wounded but still alive, and they went weeping to the Spaniards, imploring mercy, which was denied. They were cut down. Then the

An Aztec drawing showing the mounted Spaniards and their native allies attacking Montezuma's army. [North Wind Picture Archives]

Spaniards had the *caciques,* more than a hundred, who were already shackled, burned at the stakes that had been driven into the ground."

Bernal Díaz describes the same slaughter. He adds that Cortés had heard from the Indian woman who was his mistress and interpreter that the Aztecs had planned an ambush outside Cholula.

When Montezuma was told what had happened, he apparently decided that nothing would halt Cortés' march. He now prepared to meet him in awe-inspiring splendor, to shower him with gifts, and to house him and his men in the houses of his nobles.

Bernal Díaz: "When we arrived [in Tenochtitlán] we saw so many towns and villages built both in the water and on dry land, and on a straight causeway ... that we would not restrain our admiration. It was like an enchantment, because of the high towers which rose from the water. Some of our soldiers asked if what we saw was not a dream.... All was bright, with many kinds of stone with pictures that gave reason for thought. Many kinds of birds came to the lake, and I stood looking, thinking that never in the world would lands like these be discovered again."

Within days, Cortés had succeeded in having Montezuma kidnapped and brought to his own quarters. There he was chained to a seat and forced to watch fifteen of his *caciques* burned alive in front of the windows. Apparently Montezuma had now no spirit left to resist. He had vast loads of treasure brought in to ransom himself; it took the Spaniards three days to count and list it all.

Of course, Cortés had no intention of releasing the king. He had him taken up to the roof of the building in chains, a dagger pointed at his chest. The people from the city had surrounded the palace, and Montezuma begged them in tears to go away. Not long thereafter he died, either from wounds suffered on the roof or because Cortés had him strangled.

The population of Tenochtitlán had not gone away, though, and they attacked the Spaniards' houses with stones and arrows. There were in the thousands, and Cortés decided to withdraw in the night, along the causeway. The Spaniards suffered many casualties on this maneuver; many of his men fell into the lake in the dark, and drowned from the weight of the gold they were carrying.

Cortés set up camp in the countryside, and here he was soon joined by Spanish reinforcements. Most of these men had actually been sent by the governor of Cuba to bring him back, for he had sailed without awaiting the governor's permission. But when the new arrivals heard of Montezuma's treasures, they decided

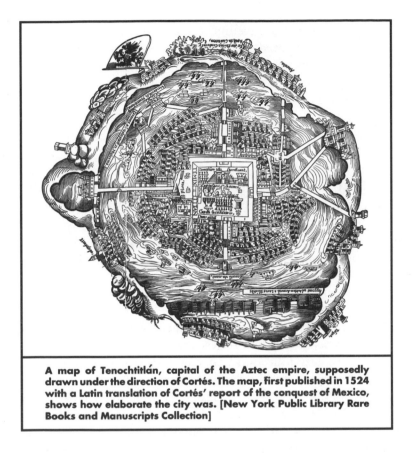

A map of Tenochtitlán, capital of the Aztec empire, supposedly drawn under the direction of Cortés. The map, first published in 1524 with a Latin translation of Cortés' report of the conquest of Mexico, shows how elaborate the city was. [New York Public Library Rare Books and Manuscripts Collection]

that it would be more profitable to enlist under Cortés than to arrest him.

Cortés now returned to the valley of Tenochtitlán. News had reached him that the Spaniards had infected the city with small-pox and that the people of Tenochtitlán were dying fast. He decided to bide his time while his troops destroyed the villages and farms of the valley, cutting off supplies to the city. And when he finally returned to the attack, it was immediately clear that the Aztecs could no longer hold him off.

A nephew of Montezuma, Cuauhtemoc, a young man of twenty, had been made Montezuma's successor. He led the defense, as the Spaniards burned down the city section by section. He was captured in the last building the Spaniards took. He was tortured to reveal where any further treasure might be hidden, but he did not speak. Cortés later had him hanged. He was the last Aztec ruler. Soon Spanish viceroys would rule Mexico.

The Mayans of the Yucatán peninsula would prove the hardest to enslave. They were subjected to the rule of two Franciscos de Montejo as governors, first the father, then the son. The father became known for feeding live children to his mastiffs. The son became known for cutting off the arms and legs of his male prisoners and for drowning the women. Parts of the interior of the Yucatán nonetheless defended their freedom until the late 1600s. Finally, they were crushed by overwhelming military might, but they never surrendered their spiritual independence and never accepted Spanish as a language they had to learn.

For the next four hundred years, Mexico was part of the Spanish empire. But the native Americans did not vanish from the face of the earth, as they did in the Caribbean. They survived as peoples, desperately poor and with no human rights, but not as imitation Spaniards or assimilated Spaniards. After independence from Spain had been won, their new masters, the *creoles* (people born in the Americas but claiming to be of European descent), treated them not very much better. They remained segregated at the bottom level of their societies, but this helped them maintain their own languages and culture. Their descendants would live to see an Indian president governing Mexico.

THE DESTRUCTION OF THE INCAS

"Peru" is the name the Spaniards gave to an empire that its inhabitants called Tahuantinsuyu. I may as well stick by the easier name Peru, but note that their Peru covered the west coast of South America from the Gulf of Guayaquil to the southern tip of the continent, an area now shared by four countries—Ecuador, Bolivia, modern-day Peru, and Chile. To the east, the land climbs ten thousand feet and higher into the wildness of the Andes mountains, which run north-south as the spine of Latin America. Wedged between mountains and ocean, Peru had been isolated for a thousand years. It was a highly organized society because its foundation, agriculture, demanded that each field receive its proper share of water and no more, and that its slopes be terraced and maintained through communal effort.

Peru was ruled by a hereditary line of kings called Incas, each one an absolute monarch and believed to be a child of the sun (as are today's emperors of Japan). But it was not a tyranny because the kings, who called themselves "shepherds," acted as such: it was a class society with precise tasks and privileges for everyone but no poverty or hunger. Its people probably traded by barter because they had no money, but there was much gold and silver, which were used for the decoration of buildings and for very fine artifacts, some of which still exist. It was this gold and silver that sealed their doom.

The Spaniards in Panama had twice made brief landings in upper Peru. Francisco Pizarro, a mercenary soldier, had been on at least one of them, and in the garden of a local *cacique* in the coastal settlement of Tumbez he had seen two trees, one made of gold, one of silver. That was enough. He borrowed money for his passage back to Spain, where he succeeded in getting the Crown's agreement to go and conquer this unknown land of precious metals. In Spain he enlisted various other marauders he knew from his own violent career, including his four brothers. He had 213 men and 64 horses; he would get reinforcements later. Like Cortés, he had from the beginning the help of an intelligent interpreter. He was over fifty years old and knew that it was his last chance to get his hands on the kind of treasure every *conquistador* dreamed of. The year was 1532.

Pizarro's first military action was a landing on the island of Puna in the Gulf of Guayaquil, where he massacred the native population, perhaps hoping that this would gave him a safe base. He and his men then set out to follow the coastal road south. He sent out scouts and was soon well informed on the state of affairs in the country. In early 1532, there had been a war between two half-brothers, sons of the previous Inca. The loser was now a prisoner in the capital of Cuzco; the winner and new Inca was Atahualpa, who was ensconced in the garrison town Caxamarca in the foothills of the Andes.

THE CAMPAIGN

Pizarro had met Cortés, and Cortés had given him his recipe for conquest: "Tell the ruler you have come to save his soul. Grab him. Set a huge ransom. Kill him at the right moment, and the place is yours." This had worked for Cortés with the Aztec nation, and it would work for Pizarro with the Inca nation too—but mostly because the Inca nation was emerging from a civil war when Pizarro appeared on the scene. Pizarro followed Cortés' advice: he marched on Caxamarca, all the while sending messages and presents to the Inca. He told him that he was a peaceful envoy of the mightiest ruler in the world, the Spanish king, and was bringing the True Faith. His way was not barred—not even when he and his men marched up the final narrow mountain paths to the garrison town, where an ambush could easily have stopped them. Today those roads still cross bottomless ravines over swaying tree bridges and it takes courage to travel them; Pizarro followed them into the unknown. Well, courage he undoubtedly had. His courage and confidence were based on the Spaniards' contempt for other races, though; he also saw his invasion as "doing the Lord's work." Of course he knew he was out to destroy rather than to convert, but human beings have a great capacity to hide a truth from themselves when it suits them.

In the town, two military barracks had been emptied for him. He immediately sent his best horsemen to prance in front of the Court (the Incas had never seen horses) and to beg Atahualpa to come and visit him. Atahualpa hesitated for a day, but then went, perhaps moved by nothing more than curiosity about the guns and cannon. He was accompanied by 5,000 of his men, all dressed in white and all unarmed.

When the Indians were inside Pizarro's encampment, he had a cannon fired and shouted, "Santiago a ellos!"—"Santiago and at them!" This was the Spanish war cry, a cry of death that perversely invoked St. James, the apostle of peace. (Santiago is the Spanish for St. James.) The Indians were all killed except for the Inca, who was taken prisoner. Cortés' recipe was followed to the letter.

And as in Mexico, Atahualpa was told to provide ransom for himself, and he did. (Even the chronicles of deeds destroying whole nations become monotonous.) Gold and jewelry were brought from the entire country, rooms were filled with gold at his command. He was not freed, however, but charged with treason in a mock trial and condemned to death. Baptized before his execution, he was given the Christian name Juan—for this took place on August 29, 1533, the day of St. John the Baptist (Juan in Spanish). Then the executioner strangled him.

DEATH OF A NATION

This highly centralized Inca monarchy, now a body without a head, was yet not subdued. All around Caxamarca the population rose. Fighting spread rapidly, fighting in which the Spaniards always ended up having the upper hand. Wood could not win against iron, staves could not win against cannon fire. And the reports of gold soon brought in a fleet of Spanish reinforcements.

Peru fell into chaos. Remote provinces continued to resist and declared themselves independent. The elaborate system of irriga-

An early representation from *La Conquista del Peru* (Seville, 1534) of the Spanish conquest of Peru, depicting an encounter between a Spanish priest and Atahualpa. [New York Public Library Rare Books and Manuscripts Collection]

tion broke down; famine and smallpox swept the land. The capital of Cuzco was burned to keep it out of Spanish hands. As soon as the Spaniards "pacified" a region, they sent the men off to work as slaves in the mines, and the birth rate soon fell to near zero. With the farmers gone, the vast fields of corn, beans, and sweet potatoes died. Coca leaves, which had only been used in religious ceremonies, were now distributed widely by the conquerors: opium for the people.

In the words of the Uruguayan writer Eduardo Galeano, "Four and a half centuries after the Conquest, only rocks and briar remain."

Conquistadores descended on the dying nation like flocks of vultures and Pizarro had to start buying off his jealous colleagues. He made his main rival, Diego de Almagro, his partner in the Peruvian enterprise, and when that did not restore peace he had him killed. Four years later Almagro's son succeeded in having Pizarro put to death. The Spanish infighting did not save the Indians. They were lost.

(One *conquistador* who got safely back to Spain with his gold was Hernando de Soto. Some years later he decided to have another go at looting America, and he returned and landed in what is now Florida. There he unloaded 600 soldiers, 200 horses, 100 man-eating dogs, and a supply of neck chains for the slaves who were to carry his gold, along with an anvil to make more chains. He criss-crossed the place, vainly looking for this gold, and marched all the way to the Mississippi, where he died of a fever and "was buried in the water"—which presumably means that his unhappy men threw his body into the river.)

European technology, European diseases, and the vulnerability of their political institutions had defeated the Inca state. Its population was *undone,* in the literal sense of the word, and it was as if its Spanish master had to repeat this undoing in each succeeding generation. The defeat continued through centuries and became an ever heavier burden.

For generations, American teachers and their students have learned of the conquest of Peru from a famous book with that title. It was written by a Bostonian, William Prescott, and published in 1868. The facts are in his book, but Prescott (like most writers of his time) never really understood what had happened: in his story, the Indians never really become human beings. He tells us that Pizarro acted "in the spirit of the knight errant." Would it had been so.

Two English agricultural specialists, Edward Hyams and George Ordish, in their book *The Last of the Incas* (1963), give us a modern view, the view of writers who have tried to think this through from the viewpoint of the victims. "Above all," they write, "a kind of paralysis was induced in the Peruvians by the unprecedented and nerve-shattering ferocity of the Europeans. They were used to war, but it was a war conducted according to strict rules [which were] relatively mild. They now found themselves opposed to a new kind of human being who waged war *à l'outrance* [to the bitter end]."

They continue: "The successful and stable paternalism of the state was now replaced by a complete disregard for the people ... not only were their barest wants not provided for, but their accumulation of wealth in stored food and cloth, in vast herds and fertile soil and carefully conserved water, was all dissipated.... The Spanish disregard of ordinary human behavior was incomprehensible to them, and it induced in them the ultimate despair, from which they do not seem to have recovered."

4

THE ENSLAVEMENT

I will not spin out the story of the many Spanish military campaigns. The Caribbean islands, Mexico, and Peru each tell the history of a different kind of defeat of the native population. Other nations provided variations on the same theme. A *conquistador* would appear, with soldiers, horses, and cannon; the local leaders would be burned alive or hanged; the people would then be enslaved. It made no difference whether the Spaniards came upon stone-age tribes, as in some remote wildernesses, upon simple rural societies, as in the West Indies, upon a highly organized state, as in Peru, or upon a priestly autocracy, as in Mexico. The military time-gap between invaders and invaded was always thousands of years.

Both the weapons and the spirit of the peoples involved were as different as if they were from different planets. Indeed, the emotional impact of the Conquest can perhaps be understood, really understood in our bones, if we think of a late night horror movie where our (more or less) peaceful towns are invaded by beings from outer space, looking like us but different, communicating in weird sounds, merciless as no human being we know of, invulnerable in their iron or leather skins, and with weapons that have captured the powers of fire and of lightning. Defeated by these invaders, we have nothing left to hope for: the Indians knew of no other world but their own, and that world had come to an end. They did not even have the desperate last comfort of the Jewish prisoners in German concentration camps who knew that somewhere far away people were fighting for their cause.

All of the Americas below the Río Bravo (the river that is called the Rio Grande in the United States) fell under Spanish occupation, except for Brazil, which was east of the Pope's dividing line and was conquered by Portugal. The Portuguese king had immediately divided up the coastal zone into large *encomiendas*, where thousands of enslaved Indians were put to work. The first Portuguese governor had announced that there were so many natives, there would never be a shortage of labor "even if we were to cut them up in slaughterhouses." He was wrong: the working conditions were such that one generation of slavery was enough to empty the plains. And as late as 1910, a prominent British historian would write that the resistance of the Brazilian Indians to the Portuguese was "a sign of their gross ignorance." (This was in the famous *Encyclopaedia Britannica*.)

A CONTINENT IN CHAINS

There was no real ending to the conquest of Latin America. It continued in remote forests and on far mountainsides. It is still going on in our day when miners and ranchers invade land belonging to the Amazon Indians and armed thugs occupy Indian villages in the backwoods of Central America.

The continued, if subdued, state of warfare suited the *conquistadores* well. Capturing Indians and making them "prisoners-of-war" made it easy to enslave and brand them. If an Indian settlement tried to surrender, it was easy enough to provoke an incident that led to resistance and produced the same result. Thus the Spaniards set about enslaving virtually the entire population—as many as a 100 million people. "King Solomon's Treasures," that mystical wealth Columbus had kept expecting, was now indeed found in gold and silver mines of spectacular richness, and it was here that the enslaved Indians were set to work.

We know precisely the shape that this slavery took, for a stream of reports went out to the Court in Spain, which had reserved a fifth of all the proceeds for itself. It must be said that its emissaries, in those reports, registered protest against the cruelties and "the waste in lives." In reaction, the Court at various times set rules meant to soften the worst abuses, but the colonists ignored them. As well they might: in the year 1601, for instance (at a time when the slaughter had lessened because of a shortage of labor), King Philip III issued a *public* decree banning the use of forced labor in the mines. Yet the same ship carried a *secret* decree spelling out that forced labor could continue if its abolition would reduce production—as of course it would. As you see, we know more about what was going on than most of the people of the time.

De las Casas traveled in what is now Guatemala. He wrote: "The Indians had to carry anchors to the coast weighing three or four hundred pounds, and they marched, shackled, those pathetic naked creatures, one behind the other, their hands clinging to the shoulders and waist of the one in front, carrying the heavy burdens on their backs. And I saw many Indians thus laden, struggling in anguish down the roads." Those "shackles" included a neck iron which was locked around each slave's neck, and when one fell down and could not get up, it was routine not to bother with unlocking the iron but instead lop off the fallen Indian's head. I am appalled at having to write this down, but closing our eyes to it does not help the dead, nor their descendants now living.

In 1979, William Sherman (not the Civil War general but a present-day historian) published a four-hundred-page study of the Spanish slavery in Central America. (It is listed in the bibliography.) In it you read about the arrival of the new Spanish governor of what is now Nicaragua. We are in the 1540s. The governor "took Indians as carriers to transport his goods to the city of Léon, including not only his personal effects but also iron bars and tools, some of which were for trading. More than three hundred loads were carried by the Indians, among whom were found those of the [former] nobility, forced by chains and iron rings around their necks. According to the town council report, the governor had left orders that any Indians who returned were to be hanged, a command that was afterward carried out. But as it happened, most of the carriers perished from fatigue and ill-treatment."

A Spanish official in what is now Honduras reported: "The Spaniards burned down towns and caused great destruction. Babies [of newly enslaved women] were tossed aside. Two hundred Indians were 'punished' [to instill terror], one-third by being burned to death, one-third by being torn apart by dogs and one-third by having their eyes plucked out or arms cut off." The official then suggested to the Crown that "guilty" Indians should be punished according to Spanish law and not in such savage ways. "The Indian *pueblos* [towns] had houses which seemed like the royal chambers of kings and lords ... some held as many as a thousand families. And all this was destroyed."

A certain Andres de Cerezeda, ordered by the Court not to take more slaves, "sought a subterfuge." He had his captives accused of crimes for which they could be exiled forever. Ships were waiting, and at the dock they were sold for axes, oil, wine, and gold. Enslaved, they were taken to Cuba, Santo Domingo, Hispaniola, and Jamaica. "When Cerezeda entered the *pueblo* of Naco, there were eight to ten thousand men, aside from the women and children, and at the time of this report [in 1539] there were not 250 Indian males left." Among the various deeds of Captain Francisco Gil, lieutenant-governor of Yucatán, we find that "he made unjust war on the *pueblos* for no more reason than to make slaves. In the *pueblo* of Tila he required fourteen caciques to appear before him and then demanded burden bearers." (*Tamemes*, or porters, these were called. Each carried as much as one hundred pounds for sixteen hours a day; they only lived a few months.) "When the *tamemes* were delivered, they were branded as slaves of war. The captain took his pick and divided the rest among his companions, whereupon of the fourteen *caciques* of Tila, thirteen were burned to death; the hands and nose of the last of them were cut off and hung around his neck, after which he was sent back to his people 'as a warning.'" That, too, had become standard practice. We already hear of it in the chronicles of Columbus and his brothers, where the Spaniards would tell such a mutilated man, "Go home now, carry the message."

When we think of the Spanish-American landscape, we must visualize roads along which the most horribly mutilated people wandered, men and women without ears and noses, and where those who had survived having their hands cut off, drank from puddles on the ground like dogs, and begged for food, until death delivered them.

The branding of enslaved Indians had also became standard practice. In 1526 a royal decree reached America that such branding had henceforth to be done in the presence of an official, and only after care had been taken to "verify" the status of the Indian. The decree said that Spaniards ignoring this could be punished by death. But nothing changed, although there are reports that one governor freed a cargo of *encomienda* slaves who were being sent illegally to the mines. Before they were shipped back to their *encomienda*, he had them branded with the word *Libre*—or "Free"—to cancel the brand of the illegal owner.

Within this cauldron of terror, the legal distinctions spelled out by the lawyers at the far-away Court—distinctions between "slaves made in a just war," "slaves who had come with a gift of land," "*tamemes*," and "vassals" (Indians who "only" had to contribute unpaid labor plus tribute), fell by the wayside. King

Philip II informed the town council of Guadelajara in Mexico that of the local Indians "one-third had been wiped out and the survivors would have to pay tribute both for themselves and for the dead." And when the mines began running out of labor, the "vassals" were forbidden to pay tribute in kind, which meant that they had to work in the mines instead.

GOLD AND SILVER

The story of the mines is the climax of the Spanish and Portuguese conquest. The mines are what it had been about. This was where all the legal decrees and inhuman horror came together—in the treasure from the mines. More than 90 percent of the exports from the conquered lands consisted of gold and silver. The gold fever that began with Columbus was contagious for three generations of *conquistadores.* Many of the new names the Spanish gave to the towns and provinces had the word *oro,* or gold, in them, sometimes only as a bit of wishful thinking. Through those dark centuries roving and plundering bands of *caballeros* ("gentlemen" is the traditional translation, but "thugs" will do) searched for El Dorado, where the houses were supposed to be built of gold. And their deadly vision came true in South America, where they discovered the largest gold and silver mines the world had ever known.

Silver, silver beyond human greed (you might have hoped) was discovered in 1545 near what is now the southern border of Bolivia. The few huts of the village called Potosí became, because of the silver rush that followed, for a short time the largest town in South America. The very word *Potosí* became a synonym for unheard-of wealth. Potosí's Cerro Rico (Rich Hill) was almost pure silver.

Potosí lay in the Andes mountains, 15,000 feet above sea level, on a barren, snow-covered cone of rock that was soon honeycombed with mineshafts. Indian men, women, and children, captured in the fields and villages of the Peruvian plain

An engraving by Theodore de Bry depicting a Spanish mine in Mexico. [North Wind Picture Archives]

below, were forced up into this frozen wasteland. Luis Capoche, a mine-owner of the time, noted that "the roads were so covered with people that the whole kingdom seemed on the move." A royal inspector, Alonso de Zurita, wrote that "the mines were easy to find, for the bones of dead Indians were so thick along the roads that one could never lose the way." The total output of the Potosí mines, from their beginning until 1864 (when they were near exhaustion), is estimated at $2 billion pre-1914 U.S. gold dollars. During those three centuries, *Potosí ate up 8 million Indian lives.* This is the most recent estimate, given in an 1981 study (it is in the bibliography). In Cuzco, 400 Spanish coca dealers sent a hundred thousand baskets, of 10 kilos of coca leaves each, to the mines each year to keep the labor force drugged. The coca was bought by the mine managers, "whom it saved much money." The church took a tax from the drug sales.

More terrible still were the mercury mines, which were not worked by private owners but directly by the Crown. Mercury, which was used to extract silver from crushed rock using the newly discovered process of amalgamation, is highly poisonous—the fumes will kill a man. Mercury penetrates the bone marrow, causing a constant shaking. In 1601 a royal decree ordered Indians to "congregate" near the mercury mines. There are descriptions of the slaves descending five hundred feet into the earth, down a series of ladders, and climbing up with bags of mercury ore on their backs, at times slipping and falling to their death. Those who surfaced were immediately sent down again. "The laborers all die within four years," one inspector reported to the king. But again and again through the sixteenth and seventeenth centuries the Spanish kings renewed the decrees covering their "Royal Mines."

Meanwhile, only forty miles from the Atlantic, in Portuguese Brazil, the "Potosí of Gold" had been found—the Ouro Prêto mines of the Minas Gerais (General Mines) district. Here gold was brought up from shafts that were sometimes 2,000 feet deep, first by Indian slaves, and, when those had perished, by enslaved Africans. "The slaves work, eat, and sleep in the gold-washing barracks," a local doctor reported around 1700. "They are bathed in sweat, their feet in the cold earth, on stones, or in water ... thus they get many dangerous diseases. Ouro Prêto eats up slaves at great speed." He is quoted in Eduardo Galeano's history, *Open Veins of Latin America.*

Six billion gold dollars' worth of loot was taken from Latin American between 1492 and 1800. If Potosí, where $250 worth of silver was produced for each dead slave, was typical, this adds up to a death list of 24 million Indians and Africans.

The sum in money is more than the total investment in European industry by the year 1800. Thus it is no rhetoric to say that the famous Industrial Revolution—which lifted Europe out of its traditional agricultural scarcity and made it all the world's master—was financed with the blood of slaves. Throughout that long procession of years and then of centuries, the kings of Spain and Portugal remained as much captives of the cruel gold fever as the most ignorant and greedy *caballero*. Now, in Potosí, you are shown the ruins of the prison where the slaves were locked up at night. It is all that is left of the wealth and the chains.

As for the Court officials, the lawyers, the priests, they kept their debate going through the centuries too. A Mexican viceroy argued that working in the mines was the best remedy for the "natural wickedness" of the native population. A Father Domingo de Betanzas proclaimed that "God condemned the whole race of Indians to perish, for the horrible sins committed in their paganism." Father García, a priest in the 1600s, announced that "the Indians have Jewish blood, because like the Jews, they are lazy, they do not believe in the miracles of Jesus Christ, and they are ungrateful to the Spaniards for all the good they have done them." The mines were the right place for them. Perhaps the final word should be left to Archbishop Linan y Cisneros, who told the world that the Indians had not been annihilated but were hiding out "to avoid paying tribute; and abusing their liberty."

We should not be surprised that priests, even archbishops, made such statements. The Spanish clergy played a sad role in this tale of blood and greed, with only a few lonely heroes to defend its honor—such as Bartolomé de las Casas and the Friar Antonio de Montesinos, who preached the famous "I am a voice crying in the wilderness" sermon in Santo Domingo (he was put on the next ship home). By the late 1600s, priests and friars were banned from the mining areas "as they were not interested in conversion but used their holy statues to smuggle out gold." Baptism never freed a slave; on the contrary, the owners of the mines and *encomiendas* defended their slave hunts as a way to gather the Indians together to listen to the teachings of the "Holy Faith." One priest reported that a *cacique* in the mid-1500s asked to be converted, and wrote that "I've told him of our Faith in the little time available." Why "little time"? After he had been baptized, "We placed him on a stake and shot him through with arrows."

At one time the Church had forbidden Christians to keep Christian slaves, but by the Middle Ages it was allowing the import and sale of slaves who were "infidels," or nonbelievers. Then there was an ominous change of doctrine: it was argued that the word "infidel" applied to a slave's *origin,* not to his religion of the moment. Being converted to Christianity could not help him if he was of the wrong race.

By the 1800s, the Spanish Americas were running out of the easy plunder of the first centuries of the Conquest. *Encomiendas,* rather than mines, became the site of enslavement. The *encomienda* Indian was tied to the land: he was a serf and could never leave. This status was extended to the next, and the next, and then the next generation. "Indians were abused but not so easily killed any more," one official explained. The steady income from the plantations allowed a new generation of landowners, "beneficiaries of the hardships of the *conquistadores,*" to enjoy "all the perquisites of the well-born in Europe."

THE OTHER SLAVES

Columbus had sent one ship carrying five hundred enslaved Indians to Spain, but after that the traffic was the other way, as enslaved Africans were shipped in ever larger numbers to the Americas. In 1790, the records show that a total of 74,000 Africans were brought to this continent in that one year; the total for that century was 2.4 million. Only half of these "lived long enough to be put to work," and their life expectancy once they landed was seven years. Jamaica alone imported a total of 800,000 slaves; only 340,000 were left alive in 1820, despite the births of those years. The figures for Haiti and Cuba are even more appalling. De las Casas was one of those who had suggested that Africans be imported "to save the Indians, as the negroes are much stronger"; he quickly confessed in writing to his terrible error in suggesting that one kind of slavery was less sinful than another. His suggestion was not what started the African slave trade, however. The king of Spain had already given out licenses for that and for the next four centuries few Europeans or white colonists questioned the practice.

This book says little about African slavery in the Americas. The reason for that is obviously not that it was a less horrifying crime than the enslavement of the native population; but in this book I must stay with my subject, the Conquest.

5

UP NORTH: VIRGINIA AND PLYMOUTH

The ocean winds decided the different fates of North and South America. Columbus, the Genoese who sailed from Spain by way of the Canary Islands, landed in the Caribbean, spearheading the Spanish Conquest. Another Genoese, who had also tried to promote the idea of reaching Asia by heading west, sailed from Bristol in England. He may even have tried more than once. He bucked the westerlies in the gray North Atlantic and came back empty-handed. But after the news reached England in 1493 that there was land out there, he was encouraged by Henry VII, king of England, to try again.

His name was Giovanni Caboto but he has gone down in history as John Cabot, and he is often mistakenly believed to have been an English sailor. In 1497 he landed on the shores of what are now Newfoundland and Labrador. Like Columbus, Cabot reported on his return that he had reached the "country of the Grand Khan." He too planted royal banners on the beaches where he set foot and "took possession" of the land in the name of his king. But his story of fog, ice, and fir trees failed the make the eyes of his royal sponsor light up, and Henry VII's only move was to give him ten English pounds for all his trouble.

Those shores and their neighboring lands still ended up as British colonies, not because of Cabot's royal banners but because once they knew, English captains from Bristol or Liverpool were able to reach North America by tacking against the steady winds from the west. Dutch and French ships also made the voyage.

In about 1540, Jacques Cartier, who set out from France, reached the present-day St. Lawrence Seaway and the Indian settlements that later became Montréal and Québec. In 1585, Sir Walter Raleigh founded an ill-fated colony in what is now North Carolina. But the first important European settlement was not until the early 1600s, when one set of English colonizers loyal to the king landed in what is now Virginia (in 1607) and a set of dissenter Puritans landed near what is now Cape Cod (in 1620). The Dutch bought Manhattan from the Manahatta Indians in 1626. In the wars that followed between these nations, England eventually won out over all comers. One reason was that the English colonists vastly outnumbered the French and Dutch. Not that that was something to be proud of, for the English emigration was largely caused by the English poverty of those who had recently been thrown off the land, "such unnecessary multitudes as pester a commonwealth," as a writer of the time nicely put it.

Unlike the Spanish and Portuguese, the English had come to stay; a further difference was that their voyages were private enterprises. The colonizers were licensed by the English Crown but otherwise largely left to their own devices. Their settlements have been described as "very large English estates but without the Manor house"—that is to say, without the local lord. As they grew, however, the government in London, as governments are wont to do, decided to get into the act, with governors, and with tax collectors.

A tug of war started, which culminated in the Thirteen Colonies' War of Independence in 1776. This was a struggle among equals—among white Anglo-Saxons, people who spoke the same language, used the same guns, worshipped the same God, and thus their battles are pretty fairly described in our textbooks. In U.S. schoolbooks you may find a mention or two of Perfidious Albion and in British schoolbooks of ingrate Yankees, but by and large it is an objectively told family quarrel, with perhaps as the only real baddie Mad King George III.

However, this book is about how the native American population fared. They numbered 10 million in what is now the United States and Canada—that is the best figure modern anthropology has come up with. Those millions were divided into hundreds of nations and tribes, with different languages and different cultures. There were nomadic hunter societies and nations with large towns and a well-developed agriculture. All of this was carefully described by some of the early European visitors, whose illustrated stories were read by a public fascinated by these new travels. Yet none let themselves be confused by the facts when the time came to justify the English Conquest as taking place in an empty wilderness where only wild beasts and "brute savages" roamed. The basic argument was always that the settlers were facing a *vacuum domicilium,* legalese for a wasteland, because the Indians had not "subdued" nature. (Such arguments sound better in Latin.) And when those Indians and their farms and fields became an undeniable presence, few Europeans had trouble convincing themselves that they were the "superior race," a "better growth," as Cotton Mather later put it, for whom the "inferior race" had to make room. (This Cotton Mather was a Christian clergyman who wrote such entries in his diary as, "Today, we sent six hundred black souls to hell," which meant, "Today we murdered six hundred Indians.")

An engraving by Theodore de Bry of Indians navigating a stream in what is now Virginia. The engraving emphasizes the abundance of fish, crabs, and turtles. De Bry never visited America; he based his pictures on descriptions, and in this case on watercolors made by an English colonist, John White. [New York Public Library Rare Books and Manuscripts Collection]

Mather had illustrious precedents: King James himself, he of the King James Bible, called the Indians of Virginia "the refuse of the world." Samuel Purchas, famous English geographer, wrote about them that "the unnatural naturals had forfeited by disloyal treasons their remainders of rights; the removal of their natural right abolished their natural existence, and Virginia became a virgin portion." Virginia had been named by Sir Walter Raleigh in honor of Elizabeth, the Virgin Queen; but what Purchas's gobbledy-gook meant was that it was now a virginal, uninhabited land. Its native population had become non-persons waiting to be "abolished," as these naturals (people living in a state of nature) had become "unnatural." How had this happened? By their "disloyal treasons," that is to say, by their waging war on the English when they did not want to (and could not) retreat any further. This is a vision which was carried through the centuries: it was voiced again—although in more moderate words—by Presidents George Washington and Thomas Jefferson. It was the vision that the Indians had no right to defend their own lands. Indians who were not "friendly" (that is, ready to be subjugated) but "hostile" deserved to be annihilated, down to the last woman and child. Military honor (something Europeans through the centuries increasingly revered) did not cross the ocean and apply to Indians. Breaking a truce, killing an envoy—all was permitted. An Indian general who lost could be hanged like a criminal. Widows and children of defeated Indian generals were sold into Spanish slavery.

WHITE INDIANS

There is a fascinating touchstone for the comparison of these two clashing civilizations: "white Indians." A New York historian, James Axtell, published a study about them in 1972: they were white people who voluntarily or as captives spent long periods in Indian societies. Axtell quotes an eighteenth-century member of the King's Council of New York: "After the peace treaty between the French and the Iroquois of 1699, few of the French captives could be persuaded to return to Canada.... The English had as much difficulty to persuade the people taken prisoner by the French Indians to leave the Indian manner of living. No arguments, no entreaties, nor tears of friends and relations could persuade many of them to leave their Indian friends. On the other hand, Indian children have been carefully educated among the English, clothed and taught, yet there is not one instance that any of these would remain, but returned to their own nations."

Benjamin Franklin says the same: "When an Indian child has been brought up among us, yet if he goes to see his relations ... there is no persuading him ever to return. But when white persons of either sex have been taken prisoners by the Indians and lived a while among them, tho' ransomed by their friends, and treated with all imaginable tenderness ... yet in a short time they become disgusted with our manner of life, and take the first opportunity of escaping again into the woods, from hence there is no reclaiming them."

Hell has no fury like a "superior race" being scorned in this manner. There was much bitterness among the colonists when the former captives maintained that the Indians were "a far more moral race," and, presumably to prove the opposite, Thomas Dale (one of the Virginia councilmen) had some young English settlers who had run away to the Indians caught and brought back. He then had them "burned, broken on the wheel,... hanged, or shot to death."

THE VIRGINIA WARS

It had started well. The Indians had kept the first visitors alive: "Their king sent us every day a brace or two of fat bucks, rabbits, hares, fish the best of the world. He sent us ... of their country corn which is very white, fair, and well tasting, and grows three times in five months. I went with seven men onto the river, the wife of the king's brother came to meet us. They set on a board wheat, venison, fish, melons ... we were entertained with all love and kindness and much bounty (after their manner) as they could possibly devise. We found the people most gentle, loving, and faithful, void of all guile and treason, such as live after the manner of the golden age." Thus wrote Arthur Barlowe, who in 1584 captained the first voyage to what Raleigh later named Virginia.

It is hardly necessary to tell you that things did not stay that way.

The history of Virginia is pretty much the history of the British colonization of America everywhere. The tale is not all unhappy. Early on there were English efforts at peace and harmony. There were a few years when Jamestown, the first settlement, seemed about to become an integrated community of English settlers and Indians of the Powhatan nation, which straddled the body of water now known as the Chesapeake Bay. Money was raised in England to build a "college" where the Indian children were to be taught "the first elements of literature," which would lead them on to Christianity and "civility." The English knew of the Indian hostility to the Spaniards in Latin America and they generally thought it well justified. De las Casas' *Destruction of the Indies* had been translated into English and Dutch, and those two nations used it as propaganda, of course, when they were at war with Spain. The English repeatedly told the Indians that they would not steal their land as the Spaniards had done. But in the end, war became unavoidable because the English would only accept the Indians on their—the English—terms. The Indians would have to accept English religion, laws, and ideas about private property; they would have to trade on English terms; and above all they would have to sell an ever increasing share of their nation. If they balked at that, then Scripture, in the example of Joshua smiting the Canaanites, gave the "precept" to destroy them.

The early Virginia years, from 1608 on, were full of a suppressed, hidden, violence. John Smith, Thomas Dale, and the other leaders were military men; Smith had been a mercenary soldier in Europe, Asia, and Africa and would later write how that experience had "taught me to subdue the wild savages in Virginia." They bullied the Indians, but they avoided military confrontation. Smith had told the king of the Powhatan—whom they also called Powhatan, like his nation—that the English had landed just to escape a pursuing Spanish fleet. One of them, Newport, had gone back to England for help and would return to take them home.

An Indian settlement in what is now North Carolina, done by de Bry from a watercolor painted by John White in 1585. In this case de Bry made the original more formal and rectilinear. Such pictures did not stop the Europeans from describing the native landscape as a "howling wilderness." [New York Public Library Rare Books and Manuscripts Collection]

Newport did come back, but he brought reinforcements instead. He also brought a new plan from The London Company (which financed and controlled the settlement): Powhatan was to receive a crown, recognizing him as head of his nation but at the same time making him a vassal of King James of England. Powhatan refused. It was now obvious that the English did not mean to leave; they had planted wheat and tobacco and built fortifications. The London Company suggested a new policy: imprison the Indian leaders and raise a new generation of them in "the English way"; exile or kill the medicine men, who were "murderers of souls." (Since conversion to Christianity did not appeal to the Powhatan, London assumed that it was their medicine men who led them to "devil worship.")

During the winter of 1609-1610, Powhatan reiterated that he wanted to trade but not "lose his country." He stopped providing food. There was much sickness in Jamestown and many died; by spring the English actually decided to leave and start a new colony in Newfoundland. Jamestown had already been evacuated when Lord de la Warr showed up with reinforcements from England, fresh supplies, and instructions to stop talking to the Indians and crush all resistance. History books have dramatized this intervention "at the last moment," but it is obvious that if the Noble Lord had been too late, nothing would have altered in the destinies of Virginia and British America.

A smoldering war started, with the Indians avoiding open combat, but before long the English abandoned all pretense of fairness. Thomas Gates lured Indians into the open by staging a music and dance show in a field, and when they came they were slaughtered. George Percy, de la Warr's second-in-command, destroyed the villages and crops and "allowed his men to throw the Indian queen's children in the river and shoot out their brains for sport." Lord de la Warr wanted to end that action by burning the queen alive but Percy said that a day of so much bloodshed should end with "an act of mercy," and he had her killed by the sword instead—thus his own report spells it out.

This total war on the English side lasted until 1614, when Powhatan gave in and signed a treaty that handed over much of his land. He had lost many men and women, including his daughter Pocahontas, who had been kidnapped by the English and imprisoned on one of their ships. She was not killed—so the story goes—because she had once saved John Smith's life. She married an Englishman, John Rolfe, aboard the ship and sailed to England, where she died seven months later. This episode, embellished where necessary, is probably all that our children remember when asked about Jamestown.

From 1614 until 1622 Virginia was outwardly at peace. That was when the plans were made in England to build an Indian college and when thanks were given to the Lord "for the happy league of peace and amity between the English and the Natives." But the hidden reality was that the rapid rise in the English population and the boom in demand for their tobacco exports put the Indians in a vice. Soon "they had only three choices" (in the words of historian Alden Vaughan, who wrote a detailed paper on these years); they could keep retreating from the coastal area, they could accept living under English rule (and English missionaries), or they could try once more to get the English to leave their nation. Further retreat would put them at war with Indian nations further inland. They chose war, a choice "occasioned by our own perfidious dealing," in the (surprisingly objective) words of Edward Waterhouse's "A Declaration of the State of the Colony and Affairs in Virginia," issued in London in 1622 and carrying reports from settlers.

The war lasted ten years. It started with a sudden attack by the Indians on the settlers: 350 men, women, and children died in what became known as the Massacre of 1622. Thereafter it was only Indian men, women, and children who were killed. "We have slain more of them," the Virginia Council declared in January 1623, "than since the beginning of this colony." The governor reported, "Our only policy is, to extirpate them." All means were acceptable. When Powhatan's successor (the king had died) eluded them, he was called to a peace parley where 200 Indians were killed with poisoned drink. The London Company drew the line at this, and admonished the governor that the Indians had to be defeated by honorable means. The council answered, "We hold nothing injust that may tend to their ruin." The colonists were divided into units, to take turns in attacking Indian targets each November, March, and July, as we can read in the *Journals of the House of Burgesses of Virginia 1619-1659.*

The fighting ended when the Indians were dead or scattered. There were other Indian nations in what is now the state of Virginia—the Chickahominy, the Nanticoke, and more. The Powhatan fate became typical for all. In 1697 the lieutenant governor of the state estimated the total number of "Indian warriors" remaining at just over 360, while the number of white settlers had grown from the 104 of Jamestown to some 60,000. The debate over whether it was better to kill the Indians or to enslave them was solved by Sir William Berkeley, who was governor from 1645 to 1652. Berkeley's recipe was to kill the men and sell the women and children into slavery; that way, extermination paid for itself.

A CHANGED PERCEPTION

When the Indians and the English first came eye to eye, the Indians were reported to be "tall, comely, the women with handsome limbs, slender arms, and pretty hands." Even though they were "heathen," they could still be seen by Englishmen staying among them not as savages but as "nature's noblemen," living in the golden age of old.

Then comes the turn-about. The Indian hosts realize that these aren't ordinary guests who are respecting the rules of hospitality. The guests aren't going home, and they're tired of camping out, they want their hosts' homes and fields. "They are occupying the fruitfullest places of the land," an Englishman reports plaintively about the Indians. Fear and greed enter the relationship, or call it economic realism. Or materialism, in all its meanings. The Indians had not planned to hand over those fruitfullest places, and the English settlers were sure that they had more right to them. Not—of course not—because they had the guns and the gunpowder, but because they—well, just because they were better. Thus, almost overnight, the Indians turned from "comely" men and women to "deformed brutes," from gentle and loving to barbarous. It couldn't be said aloud as long as there was some kind of peace, but once the fighting had started, it was no longer necessary to be discreet. The ladies and gentlemen in English polite society (as they used to call it) had known all along that Indians were "savages," "slaves," "outlaws," "bloody infidels," "barbarous and perfidious," "more brutish than the beasts they hunt," "an unprofitable burden"—to quote some of their writing.

Amazingly, the Indians' very *color* changed. In the first years, they had been described as virtually white, "little more tawney than one of ours would be if he would go naked in the south of England." Now their skins were described as having "a disagreeable color." They became Redskins. The French, while not less prone to racism and to fighting Indian wars, were more willing to stay with the concept of "noble savages." But then the French *coureurs de bois* ("wood runners") lived among them, married them, and traded in their furs, without trying to take away their land.

I am not even suggesting that the new ways the English described the Indians were conscious lies. Throughout history, people have had little trouble seeing exactly what they wanted to see. As soon as Powhatan balked at ceding more land, the settlers of Jamestown began to see the Indians as "savage and bloodthirsty and terrorizing," as they put it in their report to England. In a similar way, the English when subjugating Ireland soon made the startling discovery that the Irish were cannibals and that their mothers were eating children and the children their mothers.

In order to understand this sea change, it isn't necessary to idealize the other party. I am not idealizing the Powhatan nation, or any other Indian nation; I do not think our earth has yet seen a golden or paradisiacal age. Clearly that Captain Arthur Barlowe, back in 1584, had been a bit carried away with himself after having feasted on all the fruit and venison. But it is a bitter irony that from early on the English started accusing the American Indians of the very vices they themselves had brought with them: greed, jealousy, mercilessness, belligerency. Since the English did indeed look down upon their own disinherited at home as "unnecessary multitudes" (an attitude shared by all Europeans of wealth or power), it was hardly likely they'd manage more sympathy for the Indians, once fear and greed entered the relationship.

AND THE PURITAN WARS

The Puritans who landed at Plymouth Rock and who, with later arrivals, founded the Plymouth colony (and later the Massachusetts Bay colony), have always had a magnificent press (to use a modern expression). Here were men and women not in search of wealth but of religious freedom, who had come to found the "City upon the Hill," the earthly Jerusalem. This religious freedom, however, was one-sided: they had left England to escape its "Poperies" (as they called all traces of Catholicism), but in America they founded a theocracy where their clergy were the ruling class and where criticism of their church was forbidden. Baptists, Quakers, and other "nonconformists" were exiled and sometimes hanged. In 1637, their council drew up a list of eighty-two "blasphemous errors which are to be sent back to hell from whence they came" (as they oddly put it), and which included what most of us would consider normal and private beliefs.

It may seem odd that people who make religion so important in their daily lives would show little interest in converting the heathen, but they saw the Indians more as obstacles to their City on the Hill than as human beings. Theirs was a religion in which only the few Chosen are saved, and even the converted (the so-called "Praying Indians") were kept outside their community. Nonetheless, the early days gave some foundation for the traditional stories of mutual help and friendship. These are still celebrated yearly at Thanksgiving, though surely not by the descendants of the Indians. For the belief that the Indians were "lost creatures out of hell" and that they had been "decoyed by the Devil to live far away, in hopes that the gospel of Jesus would never come there and destroy the Devil's empire over them" soon gained the day.

John Winthrop, four times governor of the Massachusetts Bay colony, had once argued that as long as the English left the natives enough land for their use, they could lawfully take the rest. But that was before he arrived here. On American ground, he came forward with the *vacuum domicilium* angle: America was wasteland and had been waiting for the white settlers. (The epidemic of a European disease, probably smallpox, before the Puritans had arrived, was of course explained as the Good Lord making room for them.) As Winthrop sat at his table writing about this "wasteland," he could by lifting his eyes see neat Indian acres of farmland—but such details have never stopped a determined man. The settlers systematically let their cattle and pigs roam through Indian crops; since by the rules of the settlement Indians could not appear as witnesses in a court of law, no redress was available to them. The Puritan courts of law also established an elaborate system of fines, to be paid by the Indians for a long list of misdeeds. As the Indians had no money, they had to pay in land. We read of Indians being fined for "traveling on the Sabbath" and losing their land that way. Winthrop himself managed to assemble 1,260 acres along the Concord River by such means.

Thus the Puritans, those unchristian Christians (to paraphrase Samuel Purchas with his "unnatural naturals") set up an unbeatable racket, a mixture of petty harassment and bullying, of holiness and violence. It lost the Indians not only their sovereignty but also their common and private land. In an age when liberty and property were virtually synonymous, even a willingness to bow their heads and "assimilate" gave Indians no place in white society except as servants.

During the 1630s a wave of new settlers arrived and the pressure for more land became "irresistible." At least, that is what we read. If you think of the hundreds of thousands who came in later centuries, you may feel justified in thinking that the only thing that was irresistible was greed itself, greed fostered by the Europeans' firm belief that God had meant them to have it all.

In 1636 ninety armed settlers went to raid Block Island, off the coast, because a white man had been found killed on his boat nearby. (His name was John Oldham and the governor of Plymouth colony had called him "more a furious beast than a man.") When the armed party landed, they found that the Indians of Block Island had gone into hiding; they burned the villages and crops and returned to the mainland, where for good measure they burned down some Pequot villages. The English went after these Pequots and told them that they were held responsible for the murder. The Pequots had to hand over "the remaining murderers" and provide assurances about future behavior. The Pequots "obstinately" refused (in the words of an English eyewitness) and in the resulting fight several Pequots were killed and wounded, and their belongings destroyed or carried off. Thus started the Pequot War.

Of course the war didn't really start over John Oldham, who was known as an infamous character. As it was, the response to his death had led to the vast destruction of Indian dwellings and crops (which meant famine), and the killing of many Indians in the resulting white rampage. (Be it noted that there are definitely no reasons-in-fact to reserve the words "rampage" and "massacre" for Indian actions, and that the action of the whites would now be called "crimes of war," while their war itself was by its very nature "aggression" in modern terminology, its aim being the conquest of land.)

Thus the tensions caused by the "irresistible" need for more land now found their outlet. After the Pequots had retaliated with several armed raids, which killed thirty English men and women, both Massachusetts Bay and Connecticut declared "an offensive war" on them.

The outcome of such a war was of course never in doubt. It ended with an attack by John Mason and his men on the last Pequot stronghold, their settlement on the Mystic River. "We

A 1769 treaty in which Pennsylvania Indians sold their land to British colonists. Each animal figure represents one tribe. [Culver Pictures, Inc.]

must burn them!" Mason is reported as having shouted, running around with a firebrand and lighting the wigwams. "Such a dreadful terror let the Almighty fall upon their spirits that they would flee from us and run into the very flames. Thus did the Lord judge among the heathen, filling the place with dead bodies," he reported afterward.

The surviving Pequots were hunted but could make little haste by reason of their children, Mason wrote. "They were literally run to ground ... tramped into the mud and buried in the swamp." The last of them were shipped to the West Indies as slaves. It is about this time that we come upon the name of John Winthrop again, governor once more, and offering bounty money: forty pounds sterling for the scalp of an Indian man, twenty for the scalps of women and children. The name "Pequot" was officially erased from the map. The Pequot River became the Thames and their town became New London.

(When I first lived in Connecticut, I discovered a Pequot Inn in Westport and a Pequot Golf Course not far from where that nation perished; I thought that it was difficult to imagine a more appalling insensitivity. But now, twenty years later, some descendants of the Pequots have surfaced, men and women whose ancestors had found refuge with other tribes. Now there is a Pacatucket Pequot reservation, a new Pequot sovereignty that is, in Connecticut. The Pequots have built a casino on their land—with investment from abroad, for no righteous local bank was going to lend money to people with such a past—and I can but hope that the white visitors will lose their shirts.)

After the Pequots, the turn came for the other Indian nations and tribes in New England. The Wampanoags had consistently helped the settlers during the forty years their *sachem* (chief), Yellow Feather (Woosamequin), had ruled, from 1622 to 1662. It had not saved them from being inexorably pushed onto an ever narrower land base. After Yellow Feather's death, his son—"determined not to see the day when I have no country"—set out to end the hostility among the Indian nations between the Hudson and the Kennebec (a Maine river) in order to present a united resistance to the Puritans. His name was Metacomet, but the English called him King Philip.

The execution of three Wampanoags in Plymouth for killing a settler started the hostilities that have been honored by the name "King Philip's War," although they were nothing more than Indian raids followed by an extermination campaign by the whites—in the course of which all Wampanoags were massacred, followed by the Nipmucks and the Narragansets, former allies of the Puritans. When King Philip himself was killed, in the summer of 1676, all Indian power in New England had come to its end. As was routine by then, surviving women and children were sold to the Spanish slavers and King Philip's head was exhibited on a stake in Plymouth, where it reportedly could still be seen in 1700.

After the fighting, two years of smallpox epidemics ravaged the Indians who had not been in the war, and who were now reduced to "tawny pagans living in nothing more than kennels." That is how Cotton Mather described them in a book he published in Boston in 1692. Mather could always be trusted for coming up with a nice phrase on such occasions. Historian David Stannard, quoting the result of statistical studies made in 1988 and 1990, gives the destruction rate for the New England Indian nations in the seventeenth century as ranging from 82 to 98 percent.

But the deaths of the Indians did not bring about the death of racial hatred among the whites. On the contrary: "Monsters shaped and faced like men," a Boston writer called them in 1676. It was a hatred no longer based on fear but one based on ignorance. Perhaps the English needed it as a barrier against any sense of guilt. As another contemporary wrote, "The vulgar cry is now to kill all Indians when they cannot kill one."

6

THE WARS WITH EUROPE

Until the day that the Thirteen Colonies took up arms against England and fought the War of Independence, European soldiers in America had been fighting each other on behalf of their various governments—apart, of course, from fighting Indians. England had taken on France, Holland, and the Spanish soldiers, who had come not from Spain but from Latin America.

In the middle of the eighteenth century, when much of Europe was at war with itself (as usual), their Seven Years War became in America the French and Indian War. France lost its footholds in Canada and along the Mississippi. James Wolfe, a hero or a mad swashbuckler depending on your point of view (he had joined the British army at the age of thirteen), conquered Québec for England, and both he and his French opponent died in the final battle. They were given a joint monument with a Latin inscription, for Europeans of that century delighted in such military drama, straight out of the pages of Homer.

Behind the literary curtain of noble and mortally wounded opponents shaking hands, the Indian nations were lured to play their part. For them no monuments with Latin verse. The fate of the Iroquois Federation is typical. This league of "Five Indian Nations" (after 1722, Six Indian Nations) had its home in what is now New York state. Its structure of decentralized democracy amazed early Europeans. Benjamin Franklin expressed his envy of their enlightened society and translated their constitution into English; it is widely believed that it inspired some of the wording of the later constitution of the new United States. In the eighteenth century, the Iroquois Federation was recognized as an independent nation by the European powers. Early on in the European power struggle, its territory, which reached as far as Québec, was invaded by the French, and that made it the natural ally of the British: its state became a protective shield for the British against the French to the north. France in its turn sought an alliance with the Algonkian. Thus the Indian nations were sucked into the European wars. They quickly found out that there is little ritual or symbol in European warfare. The weapons of the Europeans were of course immensely superior, and when one Indian nation got them, it became crucial for its neighbors to get them also. The concept of war became "modernized," and soon Indians were fighting Indians with European weapons in European power struggles—struggles that England was bound to win since the British navy controlled the ocean and the supply lines from Europe. Of course, they also had the long-term advantage in numbers of immigrants.

Later, when those immigrants in turn waged war on England, many Indian nations of the East coast sided with the British troops against the rebellious colonists—unavoidably. By that time they saw the only hope for their own future in the policy of restraint that Britain had begun to force on its settlers. (In this century, John Collier, Franklin Roosevelt's Commissioner for Indian Affairs, would argue that precisely because Britain had begun protecting the Indians and thus infuriating the white frontiersmen, the "Borderers," it had lost the war against the colonies.)

The Iroquois, the Shawnees, the Delawares allied themselves with the British, but they hardly got a "thank you." "No matter who wins in these battles, the Indians lose," the Indian leader Pontiac had wisely said. It is interesting that the British colonists, like the French before them, never believed that the Indians entered these wars in the hope of defending their own land; it was always assumed that the "French were behind it" or the "British were behind it." In the self-same way, the United States assumed two hundred years later that the Soviet Union "was behind" the Vietnamese war. This has little to do with politics; it is a sign of that tenacious Western arrogance: natives don't know what they want unless we tell 'em. As for the members of the Iroquois Federation, their society was virtually destroyed in the battles of the War of Independence, and they now live scattered over New York state, Wisconsin, Oklahoma, and Canada.

The final chance for outside support for their cause, or so it seemed to the Indians, was the British-American War of 1812. (It was not the final chance. In our time, indigenous populations are finding an outside, international, ally in the General Assembly of the United Nations.) A Shawnee general, Tecumseh, had spent years traveling up and down the eastern seaboard trying to cement a confederacy of Indian nations that would present a unified front to the settlers. He thought that the British, who held Canada, posed no threat to the Indian lands in the old Northwest, while the American colonists did; to the contrary, the English had let him understand that they would welcome his confederacy as a valuable ally in a future balance of power. Thus Tecumseh crossed into Canada in the summer of 1812 to ally his nations with the British.

It didn't work out. England was still fighting Napoleon in Europe, and its leaders were beginning to realize that within a long-range view of the world, the United States would be a natural partner for them, not the Indians. Thus England did not fight that war to the bitter end, and let its allies be crushed. For the Indians, the end was always bitter: Tecumseh should have heeded Pontiac's words; he was killed on the battlefield. The story is told that he foresaw his death and therefore took off his British sword and the accoutrements that came with his rank as an officer in the British army, dying in what was "the only Indian uniform, a deerskin hunting jacket."

It has often been written that Tecumseh was "too late," but while the outcome might have been postponed, it was always a certainty. Within the logic of history and of the qualities and vices of the human race, it was unavoidable that the French would lose their wars, that the English would end up losing against their former countrymen, and that the Indians would lose their continent.

In the latter part of the eighteenth century, the English at home, the gentlemen running Parliament, had indeed become more enlightened toward the Indians than the English in America. But that is only a different way of saying that such enlightenment had become a luxury that London could now afford, while the colonists imagined they could not. Unfortunately, advances in humane and civilized behavior often make their appearance in history only when it is no longer so very profitable to be inhumane. The French trappers in the American wilderness had lived like friends with the Indians but they could hardly have survived otherwise; in the coming wars of independence of their Caribbean colonies (and later in North Africa), the French behaved appallingly. England, once it had become the first industrial nation, was in the vanguard of the international fight against the slave trade and slavery. It was the English liberals in Parliament who, against the opposition of their own government and their own aristocracy, pushed the anti-slavery laws through. Yet that self-same liberal, modern-industrial establishment had been founded on an accumulation of wealth produced by slavery. (In the early years of the eighteenth century, England had forced Spain into a treaty, the *Asiento*, by which it got itself a contract "to supply negroes to the Spanish colonies, 4,800 a year for a total of 144,000 in thirty years, import duties to be paid.")

INDEPENDENCE FOR ALL THE AMERICAS

Inspired by the new United States, and very much helped by the turmoil in Europe at the time, the Spanish and Portuguese colonies rose up too. The French Revolution had shaken up the old order; then came Napoleon, who shook up every kingdom and dukedom in Europe. When his armies walked into Madrid (the year was 1808), the days of Spanish authority in Latin America were clearly also numbered. There were years of fighting ahead, but by 1825 seventeen independent republics had been created out of the Spanish viceroyalties on this continent.

The word "independent" needs qualifying. One man's independence remained another man's slavery. The irony of the Latin American wars of independence was that the settlers turned reality on its head. Those children of *conquistadores* and slavers now presented themselves to the world as victims. The wars were fought by *creoles,* people of Spanish origin born in Spain but living in America, against people of Spanish origin born in Spain but living in America as emissaries of the king, controlling what was going on, and dragging away the loot. These Spanish Spaniards could afford the luxury of a certain detachment, and it had suited their "divide and rule" recipe in recent years to protect the native population—be it more in theory than in practice. Now they were labeled the Oppressors, while the *creoles* became the Victims in their fight for freedom.

It depends on the region how close to, or how far from, reality this picture was. In Latin America, the true victims, the surviving Indians and enslaved Africans, were very much left out of the reckoning. But here too, as is the rule in such upheavals, they were in demand as allies when the going was bad. Only in Mexico did they play such a large role that it lastingly changed that society. But revolution was not the right word for what was going on.

Nowhere did underdogs become upperdogs; instead, one set of upperdogs was exchanged for another.

This doesn't mean that nothing much changed. The heavy weight of Spanish bureaucracy was shattered, and without it there were no functioning institutions (very different from the Thirteen Colonies). The new *creole* leaders issued burning proclamations. Battles were lost and then, increasingly, won. There was a smell of gunpowder in the air, and a heady excitement. Breaking down the front door of some governor's mansion could smell like the taking of the Bastille. Most of the new republics began by abolishing slavery and serfdom, but when things had calmed down and there was time for some serious bookkeeping, they let it creep back in.

They had little to build new institutions on unless they were prepared to restore structures from before the Conquest. In Peru and Argentina, there was talk of electing new Incas, but that was of course just romantic nonsense; no one dreamed of giving the Indians back any authority. (The last man of royal Inca blood, Tupác Amáru, had come out for the abolition of slavery and forced labor in 1781. The Spaniards tortured him to death in the central square of Cuzco.) Brazil decided to import a refugee king from Portugal and became a monarchy. In Mexico, the *creoles* would, some decades later, try an unfortunate experiment with a Habsburg king brought in from Austria.

Perhaps the only true local rebel and liberator, in word and in deed, was Simón Bolívar. Bolívar was born in Caracas in 1783; he grew up in Europe and shortly after his return became involved in the rebellion against Spain. He spent the next twenty years, until his death in 1830, on battlefields all over South America fighting Spanish royalist soldiers. He freed what is now Colombia, Bolivia, and Peru, helped write their constitutions, accepted (and resigned from) their presidencies. He wanted to make an end to slavery but had to be satisfied with murky laws promising freedom for the *children* of slaves. He vainly tried to have the new states join in a federation. Unlike George Washington and

Thomas Jefferson, he did not believe in the right of the *creoles* to
see themselves as "the Americans," ignoring the disinherited
Indians around them. "We are neither Indians nor Europeans,"
he wrote in 1815, "but an intermediate species between the
legitimate owners of this country and the Spanish usurpers."
Beautiful words, but they were not to the taste of the men of
property who, throughout history, have wrapped their self-interest in what they are pleased to call realism. He knew they were
undermining his vision: "We will never be happy, never!" he said
near the end of his life, words that have hung as a somber
prophecy over his tortured subcontinent.

I won't record the details of all those battles and battlefields.
Many books about them await any reader interested in military
history. In those years both Spain and Portugal had virtually
ceased existing as independent nations; it was obvious that their
colonial empires would soon be lost to them. England made great
haste recognizing the new republics, because it was afraid that the
French might help Spain reconquer them. That, and President
James Monroe's "Doctrine" of 1823, which warned against any
further intervention, put an effective stop to military action from
Europe. It did not end Europe's political influence and interfer-
ence, which was powerful until 1914, when it was replaced by
United States predominance.

A SUCCESSFUL SLAVE REBELLION

One war in the Americas turned into a true revolution and was
in fact the first successful slave rebellion in recorded history: the
uprising of the slaves of Hispaniola against their French owners.
It made Haiti, in the year 1804, the second independent republic
in the Western hemisphere, after the United States. (That is, if we
are not counting a secret black republic of maroons, escaped
slaves, in the Brazilian interior, which existed all through the
seventeenth century.) Hispaniola, where in 1492 the Conquest
had begun, was the first island in the Americas, and probably in

the world, where the enslaved got the better of their enslavers. For the Arawaks it came too late, but there is some consolation in these strange workings of destiny: a conquest begun, a conquest undone, on the same bit of American soil.

The French Revolution had outlawed slavery, but Napoleon reinstated it. He lured Toussaint l'Ouverture, the man who had defeated the Haitian planters and freed their slaves, to France for "negotiations." Once Toussaint was there, he was put in prison, where he soon died. (The French prison doctor performed an autopsy and wrote a paper about "the differences between the brain of a black man and a white man.") Then Napoleon sent a fleet to try and reconquer the island for its former planters.

Records describe how the French planters had their recaptured slaves torn apart by dogs at festive public events, with a band playing to drown out the screams. On one occasion, when the dogs just sniffed at their tied-up victim, a young aristocrat jumped into the ring and cut the man's skin with his dagger, to the applause of the public; when the dogs smelled blood, they attacked. Black armies, and yellow fever, in the end defeated France. But Haiti, a black nation in a slave-owning world, was still an outcast. The United States did not recognize it until the 1840s, and thereafter repeatedly sent in the marines for long periods of military occupation.

Haiti now vies with Bangladesh for the place of poorest nation on earth, and its most lucrative export in recent years was its own blood, from blood banks where its poor sell it, a pint a week. But Haiti played its role in the independence wars. At a low tide in their affairs, Simón Bolívar and his followers found a refuge there; it was from the free Haitian nation that Bolívar set out on the final campaign to defeat the Spanish armies. Before sailing, he promised Haiti's president, Alexandre Pétion, that he would abolish slavery wherever he could. Haitian troops were then added to his forces.

Bolívar's plan for a United States of South America never had a chance. Those artificial new nationalities of Argentineans,

Paraguayans, Ecuadorans, Uruguayans, would quickly become real enough for their various new citizens to lead them into an endless series of wars against one another. Hundreds of thousands, mostly Indian conscripts of course, perished. The same was to happen in our century across the artificially drawn borders of the former African colonies.

The violence in South America during the later years of the nineteenth century is but a tale of ambitious strongmen, as futile and sordid as the bloodshed of gangs disputing their territories.

THE INDIANS UNDER INDEPENDENCE

Independence from Spain and Portugal did not help the Indians. Immigration from other countries to South America jumped, and as the economies in the new republics were liberal and "wide open," nothing stopped the immigrants from buying out the Indians at bargain-basement prices. New, huge *haciendas* came into being; they were not much of an improvement over those *encomiendas* of old: the serfs were now day laborers.

In Uruguay, the last of the Charruas Indians were exterminated in 1832. In Argentina, the Indians were pushed further and further south and the armies of its various dictators, equipped with the new repeating rifles, doomed the Araucanians, an Indian nation that had for centuries resisted first the Incas, then the Spaniards. The Indians of Patagonia in the antarctic south were wiped out, as were whole tribes in Brazil, Peru, and Colombia that were in the way of the rubber barons, the new *conquistadores* of the rubber fever that started in the 1870s and lasted half a century.

The free cattle raisers of the Argentinean pampas, the *gauchos*, part Spanish, part Indian, part *mestizo* (that is, of both Indian and Spanish ancestry), did not fit into these new republics either. "Use their blood for fertilizer, it's all they have that is human," a famous Argentinean writer of the time wrote to the president of the country. (He was often quoted, but I shall leave him nameless.) Through the following years, the *gauchos* were turned into impoverished peasants, working for a miserable wage under hostile landowners. "Instead of leather boots, they now wear frayed sandals, and those men, producers of meat, have lost the right to eat it themselves," Galeano wrote. In those days the lowly lost their independence once more: they had to carry passes handed out by the landowners, and if they didn't, they were whisked off to serve in the army. How easily those gentlemen, surrounded by the comforts of civilization which they or their fathers or their grandfathers had acquired through robbery of the poor, looked down on these poor in their bare feet and rags, and deduced that they were not quite human!

Not all *gauchos*, not all the lowly, bowed their heads. The *montoneras* in Argentina, like the *cangaceiros* in Brazil, were rebel outlaws, folk heroes, protectors of the Indians. All through the nineteenth century, Indian resistance never ceased, until in our own days it found new strength. I will return to that.

AND THE CASE OF MEXICO

Mexico fared differently after its independence war began. In the early years of the nineteenth century Mexico was neither a nation of Europeans, like Argentina, nor a nation where a small *creole* elite floated miles above a desperately poor Indian underclass, as was the case in Bolivia and Colombia and Peru. Mexico became the foremost *mestizo* country, a land where the majority of the people had the blood of both the invaders and the resisters in their veins. Somehow, what has been called the "easygoing despotism" of its viceroys was harsh enough to stop the Indians from becoming assimilated Spaniards, but not too brutal to prevent large-scale intermarriage.

When the Mexicans started their long rebellion against their rulers, it was the *mestizos* and the Indians, not the *creoles*, who led the fight. The signal for the first uprising was given by the village priest Miguel Hidalgo, who rang his church bell on the morning of September 16, 1810, as if to summon the Indian villagers to mass, and then told them that the time had come to overthrow the cruel government of the Spaniards. Hidalgo's village is called Dolores, and his words of that day have become engraved in Mexican history as "El Grito de Dolores," the "Cry from Dolores." But *dolores* is Spanish for pain or suffering, and for years I thought that it meant the "Cry of Pain"— which is exactly what it was. Hidalgo's life ended on the Spanish gallows. The battle went on. By 1821, the last Spanish soldiers had been chased from the Mexican mainland.

7

HOW THE WEST WAS LOST (AND WON)

It would help our faith in human progress if the new, republican, and democratic United States had started acting more decently toward the Indians than the British monarchy, but it was not to be. George Washington became known in Indian country as "the town destroyer," having ordered the obliteration of settlements of Mohawk, Onondaga, Cayuga, and Seneca—members all of the Iroquois Confederation. I knew that Jefferson and Washington had been slaveowners; I did not know that Washington had written in 1783 that Indians and wolves "are both beasts of prey, tho' they differ in shape."

We can deal with such statements by the thought (and by telling our children) that they show that we as human beings have progressed since those days. Very few of us would now think what two hundred years ago this wise and prominent man apparently did not hesitate to announce. The easier course, and the traditional one, is to sweep such words under the rug lest they hurt our "national pride." Every child needs to find pride, and a sense of self, in the history of her or his country, but the best source of such pride may be the courage to see the truth.

The early colonists had refused to recognize the Indians' natural right to defend their land, and nothing had changed. If anything, European civilization had become more militaristic in the meantime. Europeans were conquering the world, with the best of motives, of course—this was called the "white man's burden." The "colored races" weren't subjugated (as you might have thought) through lack of machine-guns; no, it was lack of "manliness": a British military man wrote in the *Encyclopaedia Britannica,* "The Egyptian would make an admirable soldier if he only wished to kill someone!" Yet if fighting for one's country was not only a right but a sacred duty for a citizen of the United States, Germany, Russia, or England, it turned an American Indian into a "savage," and "when dealing with savages, no question of national honor can arise," as a Commissioner for Indian Affairs in Washington put it as late as 1872.

Strength, military strength that is, became equated with superiority in every sense, and before long it was no longer necessary to talk about Christians and heathens or about the tasks assigned by God to the inferior races. Science, or rather the pseudo-science of "social Darwinism," would do the job. Charles Darwin's *Origin of Species,* published in 1859, had confronted a startled world with the theory of evolution. Through thousands of years of evolution a more efficient species of butterfly may replace a less efficient species. Social Darwinism—or Darwinian evolutionary theory applied not to biological species but to human societies—jumped into the fray and (more or less) told us that the "superior" Europeans not only had the right to replace various "inferior races," but that it would be going against nature not to do so. The inferiority in question really boiled down to—no matter what reasons were given—a failure of such civilizations to have developed the arts and tools of war sufficiently, or to have copied them quickly enough from the West. Thus the *innocent* evolution of biological species through eons of time in nature was equated with the acts of will by which conscious human beings within decades exterminated other human beings who seemed an obstacle to their ambitions.

THE INDIAN REMOVAL

The new United States opened its gates to all European comers without consulting the original inhabitants of this land. The interests of those new immigrants became the interests of the republic. It might have been argued that there was room for all, but that wouldn't have pleased them in the least. They felt that there wasn't: there was no room for the Indians.

In 1828 Andrew Jackson ran his presidential campaign on his record as an Indian fighter. He stated that all Indians east of the Mississippi had to be killed or moved across the river. Here was one campaign promise that was kept. A year after his inauguration, on May 28, 1830, Congress passed the Indian Removal Act with only a few Eastern senators and representatives arguing that it was a violation of our treaties and honor. Jackson had the solid support of the southern and western states. In essence, the act provided for the deportation of all remaining Indians to what later became the state of Oklahoma. I must add (it is often left out of accounts) that individual Indians were officially given the option to sever their ties with their tribes, to stop being Indians, in which case they could stay behind and get a piece of land. The records show, though, that even this option, which would now come under the United Nations' definition of genocide, was largely a paper one. The Indians who tried to accept it found that federal officers as a rule wouldn't register their choice, or that threats, forgery, theft, or other tricks cost them their holdings.

The irony was that the Indians immediately affected were precisely those who had agreed to hand over most of their territory and who had learned to survive as farmers, who had created a written tribal language, who sent their children to school, and who were governing themselves under a constitutional tribal model not a bit inferior to that of their European neighbors. They were the so-called "Five Civilized Tribes"—the Creeks, Cherokees, Chickasaws, Choctaws, and the Seminoles of Florida (which had been taken over from Spain in 1821). By no stretch of forked tongue or pen could any of the reasons usually given by the colonists—the "needs of civilization," "empty wilderness," "hostile savages"—justify the deportation of these nations from what remained of their ancestral lands. It is this policy of leaving your victims no real chance to comply, no *out*, that turns tyranny into genocide. And it is sad and pathetic, and crying for redress, to look back on the painful seriousness with which these five nations had tried so hard to become "acceptable" to the invaders of their land.

(When I write that Florida was "taken over," I know full well that the usual form is that the United States "bought" it from Spain, just as the United States "bought" Louisiana and a lot more from France, and Alaska from Russia; and then we're usually told that the United States only paid a penny an acre, or whatever. But what was bought from those countries was of course only their presumed right to interfere. None of them ever owned or even controlled the lands they "sold" to the United States.)

Even before Jackson's inauguration, several states were ignoring the federal Indian treaties and had given themselves jurisdiction over Indian land. On top of that they made it illegal for an Indian to testify in court against a white man who had dispossessed him. Once the Removal Act was in force, Choctaws, Creeks, and Chickasaws were deported, with a great loss of life on the way, to Oklahoma, "Indian Territory" as it was called, although it was never really organized as such or given a territorial government. Their new land was once again promised to them in perpetuity, as had been the land they were deported from.

Commissioners from Washington, D.C., "negotiating," that is, dictating terms, to Indian delegates. [Culver Pictures, Inc.]

But the Cherokees refused to go.

The Cherokees went to court and argued that, precisely to retain their sovereignty over what remained them, they had freely given over large segments of land "since time immemorial theirs." The case reached the Supreme Court in 1832, and Chief Justice John Marshall ruled in their favor. He found that the United States was the legal heir to the British Proclamation of 1763, which established the Indian nations as "distinct and independent political communities retaining their natural rights." Moreover, in 1785 the United States had confirmed them in their possessions. No state could infringe on these rights.

And then President Andrew Jackson spoke the terrifying words, "John Marshall has made his decision—now let him enforce it."

The Supreme Court has no private army. The law in this country is helpless, and useless, if the President decides to sabotage it. Shortly after the Supreme Court verdict, the state of Georgia distributed the Cherokee land by lottery among the new settlers, evicted the Indians from their homes, and sent them, first to stockades all over the state, and then west under armed guard, on "The Trail of Tears." That name is no sentimental exaggeration. Of the 20,000 Cherokees (1,000 had gone into hiding in the Carolina hills), many died on that trek: the estimates I found ranged from 4,000 as the lowest, to 8,000 as the highest. (Comparisons with events of our time are tricky and sometimes odious. But perhaps it helps us realize the enormity of this crime if we see a parallel in the infamous Bataan "death march," which Japan forced our captured soldiers to go on in 1942. That is the comparison drawn by historian David Stannard, and he points out that at Bataan there were no women or children, while on the Trail of Tears they were the majority.)

The promised "perpetuity" of the new Indian Territory of Oklahoma lasted forty years. From 1866 on, the Civilized Tribes were forced to accept for settlement, first the freed slaves who had no home after the Civil War, then other Indian nations deported from as far away as Washington, California, and Arizona. And, last and not least, settlers of European descent. The different Indian nations, dragged there like dogs by a dog-catcher, had different languages and different customs. There were Nez Percé from the far northwest, Modoc from California, Pawnee from Nebraska, Ponca, Saux, and Fox, Potawatomi, Apache, Northern Cheyenne, Comanche—if you draw their trails of tears, you get a web covering the entire country, with its centerpoint in Oklahoma. *How dared people do this!*

Those varied nations had been surprisingly successful at collaborating (well, they had little choice), and plans were made by

The famous chief, Geronimo, third from right, with other Chiricahua Apaches outside a prison train bound for Florida. The year is 1886. [National Archives]

their council for the creation of a free Indian state with its own government. But no, that was not the end of the story. In the spring of 1889, most of the area was declared open to homesteaders—European immigrants who were awarded land in return for the promise to farm. They had been waiting at the border, ready to grab the best pieces. By 1904 the entire "Indian Nation," except for a tract in the northeast, was opened to immigrants; in 1907 Oklahoma became a state of the union. "Perpetuity" had come to its final resting place.

Many documents had been exchanged and many treaties signed while it lasted. In the words of Alexis de Tocqueville,

"The Spaniards were unable to exterminate the Indian race by those unparalleled atrocities ... nor did they even succeed in wholly depriving it of its rights; but the Americans of the United States have accomplished this twofold purpose with singular felicity, tranquilly, legally, philanthropically.... It is impossible to destroy men with more respect for the laws of humanity." He wrote those words in 1835. We know now that the Indians of Oklahoma were not destroyed; a number survived, as did the core of their culture. In 1990, the census counted 250,000 Indians in Oklahoma, 8 percent of the population. This is, of course, more a testimony to their endurance than to the good faith of the government.

As for the fifth Civilized Nation, the Seminoles, they too refused to be moved. They didn't go to court, they went to war. Once the word *seminole* meant *runaway* in the Creek language. What are now called Seminoles was a tribe of the Creek nation that fled to the bayous and swamps of Florida to maintain their freedom; there they were joined by "runaway" southern slaves, and from 1810 or so on, those two groups had jointly fought various U.S. army expeditions sent to catch the former slaves and to subdue the Indians. Such men were not going to let themselves be herded away: the Seminoles held out from 1835 until 1842 against a pride of U.S. generals and battalions. This was the longest and most bitterly fought U.S.-Indian war.

In the last months of 1837, a Seminole general, Osceola, asked for negotiations leading to a truce. U.S. Brigadier General Joseph Fernandez accepted. But when Osceola showed up, Fernandez had him taken prisoner and sent to a fort in South Carolina, where he soon died. The war continued for four more years and ended with the deportation of the surviving Seminoles. The U.S. troops also recaptured and re-enslaved five hundred runaways, men and women, and it was said that the capture of each one of them had cost the U.S. army $80,000 and the lives of three soldiers.

WEST OF THE MISSISSIPPI

President Jackson's Removal Act basically meant (if you leave out what de Tocqueville called the tranquility, legality, and philanthropy) a choice between removal or extermination. But for many the fate in store would be both: first one, then the other.

Indian resistance east of the Mississippi ended with the Seminole war, but in the lands west of the great river an inrush of new immigrants meant new wars and new miseries. In 1846, the United States declared war on Mexico; after two years in which both sides competed in snafus, courage, and incompetence, the U.S. artillery decided the issue, and at the 1848 peace conference, Mexico lost half its territory to the United States. That unlocked Texas and California to the European immigrants; the 1848 California gold rush sent an avalanche of fortune hunters to the west coast, over land and by ship around Cape Horn. Once more, gold fever was sealing the doom of native Americans.

The rich coastlands of what is now the state of California had been home to a prosperous population of Indians; a wealth of different tribes and nations and civilizations found their food supply by fishing, especially for salmon. The first onslaught came with the Spanish missionaries and their mission settlements. Those missions, run first by Jesuits and then by Franciscan monks, are supposed to have been well-springs of civilization and Christian love, and at any high-society function in Santa Barbara you may find yourself standing next to a lady or gentleman who still believes that's how it was and who proudly traces his or her line all the way back to the Spanish *hidalgos*. It's a moth-eaten myth, though, and even the 1911 *Encyclopaedia Britannica* calls the Indians at those missions "virtual slaves." An 1817 Russian traveler (Vasilu Golovnin) described their quarters as "worse than cattle pens" and their mortality rate as staggering.

After the United States took over, the Indian death rate continued to climb. By 1880, some 20,000 California Indians were left of what was, at the lowest estimate, the 350,000 who lived there before 1492. "They were shot down in cold blood, their squaws raped [by the gold rush arrivals]," General George Crook wrote, reminiscing of the days when he was a lieutenant in a California frontier town. "We had to witness the treatment of them without the power to help.... Then, when they were pushed beyond endurance and would go on the war path, we had to fight them." Lieutenant Crook's insight did not keep him from opting for a career as an Indian fighter.

In the midwestern plains, the Indians came to their deaths in similar ways, with starvation as an added weapon. The federal government supported the slaughter of the buffalo herds (60 to 80 million were killed), as this would undermine the new societies of the hunters of the plains, the Sioux and Cheyenne. I use the word "new" because they had adopted the European horse and the European rifle in a new way of life. Once the transcontinental trains were running, finishing off the buffalo and gaining military control of the prairies was easy. Starvation forced the Indians into wars that were lost almost before they had begun ("Massacres of Indians rather than wars," the *Encyclopaedia Britannica* comments). Survivors were taken to Oklahoma as prisoners-of-war.

One of the lowest points in these bloody years was the Colorado bloodbath of 1864, when Sand Creek, an unarmed Cheyenne village, was wiped out by a Colonel John Chivington. Its people, at the time mostly women and children, were securely at peace with Washington and were flying an American flag for their protection. But Chivington had gone on record as telling his soldiers, "Kill and scalp them all, little and big, *because nits make lice.*" Those words have since given him a bad name, but militarily speaking, he wasn't out of line. His former commander-in-chief and president, Andrew Jackson, was still alive; Jackson had told the nation, "If you pursue a wolf, you have to kill the whelps too." General William Tecumseh Sherman, he of the Indian middle name, told Congress in 1867, "Carry the war to the Indian camps where the women and children are.... Punish all Sioux to the extent of utter extermination if possible." (A hundred years later

I heard arguments for killing Vietnamese children because "They'd just grow up to be communists and fight us.")

When Chivington's attack on Sand Creek was over and the Indians dead, he sent a message that he had won "one of the most bloody Indian battles ever fought." At first it seemed as if deeds such as this were no longer acceptable: a Congressional inquiry followed, a senator came to Denver, Colorado. But the senator reported back that when a public hearing was asked, "Should Indians be civilized or exterminated?" a chorus of shouts arose in the auditorium, "Exterminate them! Exterminate them!" Not surprisingly, then, nothing came of the inquiry. Chivington became a popular lecturer on "Indian policy."

The Sand Creek killings were one case in many. But for one brief moment Sand Creek became notorious and in a nation engulfed in a deadly civil war, there were yet some people who found their voice and protested. It is easier to focus on a single crying injustice than on the amorphous and almost abstract evil of an "Indian policy." When I think of the book by Bartolomé de las Casas, I think of the Indian boy who appeared in a clearing in the woods with his parrot, and the Spaniard who simply drew his sword, beheaded the boy, and continued on his way with the parrot. When I think of Sand Creek, I think of the small Indian boy who crawled out of a trench on the morning after the slaughter, mysteriously alive, and of the U.S. army major standing nearby who pulled out his pistol and shot him through the head.

The voices of protest were not heard in Colorado, where the new Americans had convinced themselves, as once the Spaniards had, that Indians aren't people.

A MIRROR OF THEIR MINDS

The popular fiction of the United States in the mid-nineteenth century reflects very nicely how many people were thinking. In vastly popular novels, Indians were killed like flies by a hero who had as a rule one faithful and comic black retainer in his wake, and maybe one "civilized" Indian, sad and no longer dangerous. These works may have been seen as entertainment, but they certainly made political points: in one of them, the hero (or better, the author, James Paulding) announces, "It seems only necessary for a bloody Indian to massacre and scalp women and children to gain immortal honor; he will be glorified by authors, philanthropists and petticoated petitioners." In other words, "We are much too *nice* to the Indians." (Such passages in their unfunny and false irony hit the same note as some columnists in our day when promoting the Vietnam war.) Paulding's output sold like the traditional hotcakes. Even more popular was William Simms, whose *The Yemassee, An American Romance,* was the *Gone with the Wind* of its time.

Yemassee has an Indian-hunting hero, Harrison, who in the end turns out to be the state governor in disguise. Apparently the governor had got sick of the wishy-washiness of the Indian-loving politicians in Washington. But the true hero of the book is Harrison's dog Dugdale, a direct fictional descendant of the man-eating mastiffs of the Spaniards. Harrison has trained Dugdale to kill Indians, using a stuffed figure painted to resemble a Redskin and made more appetizing "by deer's entrails hanging around his neck." Harrison is fighting an Indian and shouts, "Dugdale!" and next we get a detailed description of how the dog jumps to it and bites through the Indian's neck. Perhaps you can only truly appreciate such a scene if you have first shivered (or drooled) over a preceding one where a dusky savage espies a pure, white, young women, innocently asleep, and then, just in time... *Gone with the Wind* has little to do with what really happened in and after the Civil War, but it surely shows how many people like to think of it; presumably *Yemassee* did the same for the Indian wars.

LAST OF THE FREE SIOUX, LAST OF THE FREE CHEYENNE

The Sioux and Cheyenne managed to cling to their traditional ways for a few more years after the coast-to-coast railroad was completed in 1869. A year earlier, the Sioux had managed to negotiate a treaty with the United States that left them in possession of half of what is now South Dakota and part of Wyoming, their old hunting grounds, which still held enough buffalo to feed and clothe them: this was the 1868 Treaty of Ford Laramie, which also saved the Paha Sapa, the sacred Black Hills, for them. It was the last formal treaty between the United States and an Indian nation. In 1871 Congress banned any future treaties: from then on they were simply called "agreements," and the government was as little hamstrung by these as it had been by the more formal treaties.

In 1875, General George Custer (or Colonel Custer—his army rank went up and down through the years) led an expedition through the Black Hills despite the treaty. Custer reported gold in them hills, and the usual gold-rush savages soon made their appearance. For a brief time President Ulysses Grant (unlike Andrew Jackson with the Cherokee) tried to use the army to keep them off Sioux land. But by 1876, with thousands of miners or aspiring miners "trampling through the muddy streets" of the new frontier town, Custer City, and pushing toward the southern hills, the army was withdrawn. The Indians refused to accept the government offer ($6 million) for the sacred hills—"I will sell no land of ours to the white man, not even a pinch of dust," Sitting Bull answered. The government then declared the territory open to the waiting whites and ordered the Indians onto reservations.

Even if the Indians had wanted to obey, they couldn't: it was mid-winter. The soldiers who were sent against them could not set out until spring had come. It was June when General Custer rode his men to Little Big Horn mountain, where he was defeated by the Indian general Crazy Horse, and—in the words of the Sioux writer Vine Deloria—"died for our sins."

The news of the defeat of a U.S. general "at the hand of savages" reached Washington one day after a Fourth of July full of flags and speeches, and it created, or was made to create, the "national outcry" customary at such occasions. A vast military force was sent out. The Treaty of Fort Laramie, broken by the United States, was now declared as to have been broken by the *Sioux*. In the autumn of 1876, the Sioux and Cheyenne, defeated in a series of battles, capitulated. They were herded onto reservations, first to the stone desert of the Badlands along the Missouri River, later to the Pine Ridge and Rosebud reservations, which are on the border of what is now Nebraska. Crazy Horse never surrendered. He came of his own free will to a meeting at Fort Robinson, Nebraska, where he was murdered under mysterious circumstances.

THE INDIAN TWILIGHT

In the twilight now descending over their nations, the Indians began to seek comfort in ancient myths. The Sun Dance and the Ghost Dance would bring them supernatural help and restore their dead fighters and buffalo back to life; the whites would be eradicated; the earth would be renewed. Think of the despair those men and women must have felt when their world had come to an end and nothing but a mystery might save them. Think of the despair Indian children must feel even now when they are told their history. The unearthly help did not come. The dances were banned by the U.S. government as soon as it learned of them: they were seen as a dangerous incitement.

On December 29, 1890, a U.S. cavalry contingent surprised a group of Oglala Sioux on their way to seek refuge in the Pine Ridge reservation in the middle of such a ceremony. There were two hundred men, women, and children, and their leader was one of the few surviving traditional chiefs, Big Foot. The soldiers surrounded them and began, at gunpoint, to search them for weapons. A young Indian fired a shot and immediately the troops

Big Foot in death, photographed at the Wounded Knee battlefield on December 29, 1890. [Smithsonian Institution]

opened fire from all sides, killing every Sioux, as well as a number of their own who stood facing each other. The cavalry were from the same regiment as Custer and his men; they would be awarded twenty Congressional Medals of Honor, although their only danger and their only casualties had come from the crossfire of their fellow soldiers.

This happened at Wounded Knee, South Dakota, and it was the last "act of war" of the U.S. army against the native inhabitants of this country. It should not really have been dignified with that name, I would think: two hundred men, women, and children had been shot down!

It had been a long and bitter path, across a continent, from Opechancanough who died in Jamestown near the Atlantic Ocean, to Big Foot who died in the western plains.

PINE RIDGE, A CENTURY LATER

The Pine Ridge reservation was to re-enter this nation's consciousness almost a century later, when Wounded Knee was occupied by Oglala Sioux, who later called on the American Indian Movement to help them. AIM was an organization of young Indian activists filled with 1960s plans and dreams. They were besieged by the FBI and the army. In the gunfight that followed, two FBI men were killed; Leonard Peltier, a Sioux/Ojibwa, was sentenced to life in prison for their murder. The judge, in an unprecedented legal move, has since let it be known that the President should pardon Peltier. I will get back to this.

The reservation, what I have seen of it, is a barren, miserable stretch of land with not one full-grown tree in sight, the kind of place where people must almost unavoidably "suffer from despair and apathy, poverty and unemployment, alcoholism, and the random angry violence that besets the depressed Indian communities to a degree almost unimaginable to most Americans." I am quoting Peter Matthiesen, who wrote about Wounded Knee and about those one hundred lost years in his book *In the Spirit of Crazy Horse*.

Near Pine Ridge, in the western approaches to the Black Hills, the faces of four of our presidents are chiseled into the rocky slope of Mount Rushmore. Why an area sacred to the Indians was chosen for this, I can only guess. The last of the faces cut out here, "to endure until the rain shall wash it away," as its sculptor put it, was that of Theodore Roosevelt, he who called the slaughter at Sand Creek "on the whole as righteous and beneficial a deed as ever took place on the frontier."

You might think that the Conquest of America, as far as the United States was concerned, was now complete. You'd be wrong, though. The Indians of the United States were now concentrated on a land base roughly 6 percent of what they originally had, and much of that land was arid or desert. The U.S. population in 1880 was 50 million (as compared to almost 250 million now). You might think that the Indian landholdings of 1880 would be respected: there was so much room. But you'd be wrong.

8

GUNS TO LAWS

A turning point in the U.S. government's tactics, though, came even before the final slaughter at Wounded Knee. It was the passing of the General Allotment Act of 1887.

It was a turn from violent to non-violent, but I do not mean that it was a turn from bad to good. Things were more complicated than that. There are non-violent ways that do as much damage to people's souls as bullets do to their bodies. In 1887 Americans of European origin, and the "white race" in general, were still mired in that particular arrogance that assumed that any other race had no higher destiny than to copy the whites. Thus even among the most enlightened of them in this country, it came as a *given* that true enlightenment lay in a policy of Europeanization: assimilation of the Indians with the settlers from Europe.

The U.S. "Congress of Confederation" had in 1787 passed the Northwest Ordinance which spelled out: "The utmost good faith shall always be observed toward the Indians." Yet a century later bad faith remained the ultimate moving force. Removal no longer served a purpose because the white settlers were and wanted to be *everywhere*. Extermination had killed most of the Indians once living in what was now the United States, and it was now no longer acceptable as a principle; and (if you want to be realistic) it was no longer needed. What was left? Assimilation.

The 1871 congressional ruling against further treaties meant that the Indians were to be seen as wards of the government, housed on reservations, and fed and clothed by the government—by necessity, since their economic bases had been destroyed or taken away. All this was to be controlled by government agents from the Bureau of Indian Affairs, or BIA.

(The Bureau of Indian Affairs is now under an assistant secretary within the Department of the Interior in downtown Washington, DC. It used to be under a Commissioner for Indian Affairs, but not much has really changed. The crucial decisions on land and water rights are now made in the office next door, the Bureau of Land Management, which means there is a built-in conflict-of-interest which rarely works in favor of the Indian cause.)

A CENTURY OF DISHONOR

A Century of Dishonor was the title of a book published in 1881 about the hundred years of U.S.-Indian confrontation. Its author Helen Hunt Jackson created a stir, not much less than the one created by Harriet Beecher Stowe when she published *Uncle Tom's Cabin* in 1852. On her title page, Jackson quoted Horatio Seymour, former governor of New York: "Every human being, born in this country or arriving here from any quarter of the globe, can find protection in our courts, everyone that is except those to whom the country once belonged."

But Jackson's solution to the *Indian problem* was that the Indians were to be "civilized," assimilated into the economy through land-ownership and education. This was a notion not only accepted by those who wanted to promote the Indian cause, but even more eagerly by those who were waiting to "assimilate" the land the Indians still held, and never mind the Indians themselves. (Whenever a nation or ethnic group finds itself called "a problem," it is in very great danger. Throughout the sixteenth century, Spain was discussing its "Indian problem." The Germans in this century discussed at length their "Polish problem" and their "Jewish problem." Indians may be assumed to feel that whites were their problem, but I have never seen the question of the "whites problem" raised.)

The 1880s combination of goodwill, guilt feeling, and old-fashioned greed came together into the 1887 Allotment Act, which was helped through Congress by Senator Henry Dawes. Dawes told the senators and the nation that the Indians' handicap was their "communism." They had to learn "selfishness, which is at the bottom of civilization." Three hundred years earlier the Indians had their land taken away because they hadn't subdued nature; now they were to lose it for not being selfish enough.

Under the Dawes Act (as it has since become known), the tribal reservation lands were to be allotted to individual Indians and to Indian families. Every male Indian head of family was to receive 160 acres (one quarter of a square mile) on the reservation—under a kind of trust system, though, where he had to prove over no less than twenty-five years that he was worthy. Single people and orphaned children were to receive lesser pieces. Once that had been done, any "surplus" would be bought at bargain-basement prices by the government, for distribution among white immigrants under the Homestead Act. And, surprise, a surplus was found—in fact, a very large surplus. The land a tribe or nation held in common was thus "legally" expropriated, and the members of the tribe were turned (on paper) into small farmers. One of the congressmen who voted against this sting operation said, "If this were done in the name of greed, it would be bad enough, but to do it in the name of humanity ... is infinitely worse."

Students, dressed in "American" clothes, at a government Indian school on the Swinomish reservation in the state of Washington, in the early years of this century. [Culver Pictures, Inc.]

A majority of the native Americans of the time wanted to live within the framework of their tribal communities, and the records show (and most Indians whom I know confirm it) that this is still so. The consumer society did not lure them then and it still does not lure them, after a century of ads and films and lastly, television. There were many other flies in the Dawes ointment. Congress voted $30,000 for the capitalization of the new farms, something like $10 a farm. "They obviously believe in agriculture but don't believe it needs capital," a report at the time said. Thus it came about that many Indians sold their allotments as soon as it was legal and the total loss of land even surpassed the so-called surplus. By 1934, when the Dawes Act was finally declared invalid, the Indian nations had 48 million acres left out of the 138 million they had occupied in 1887. Of those 48 million acres, 20 million were on arid land where little could be grown. Presumably the Indians had also had a very clear, if expensive, lesson in selfishness.

It hadn't been all greed wrapped in hypocrisy; some of the lawmakers had the best intentions. But they failed to see how strong the forces inimical to the Indians were, how powerful the people who still and only wanted them out of the way. Those men were so much stronger than their victims—not in guns this time but in money, legal tricks, connections in Washington. They turned any law or measure inside-out and made it work for them.

The well-intended folk had imagined that the happy ending to all the blood and tears would come when the Indians vanished into the American nation, the same way the Irish, the Italians, and the Russian Jews were supposed to vanish into the "melting pot." But all this vanishing never happened. Most European immigrants entered the mainstream not as individuals but in groups. How then could it have worked for the Indians? To the contrary, those Indians who kept their ties with their reservations did well when they ventured forth into the rat race of the wider society. Those who had been cut off from their roots got stuck on the most miserably low level of the society they entered.

Single incidents reveal the suffering hidden behind the land-loss figures. The White River Utes set off on a vain crusade into South Dakota to try and find a new place where they could live as a nation. The Kichapoos signed the allotment contracts without realizing what they were doing (that was part of the sting) and then gave their land money to a lawyer who promised he'd buy them a new tribal territory in Mexico, but who absconded with the funds. As late as 1912, 2,000 Cherokees refused to accept the land money. The Lakotas fought the allotment idea until 1914.

All in vain. The steam-and-iron, dog-eat-dog, early capitalist United States had to get rid of that thorn in its side, the Indian notion that the earth is our common property, our Mother. Now the railroad barons and the oil barons and the various other industrial barons could get on with it, without tribal demands gumming up the works.

THE NEW INDIAN WARS

Allotment broke up the Sioux nation and allowed settlers into the middle of their lands. With the Allotment Act came a closer watch over Indian lives by the Bureau of Indian Affairs, which moved their children to boarding schools, willy or nilly. In those schools only English was spoken. The Sun Dance had been banned and performing it made into a felony. All this would today come under the United Nations' definition of cultural genocide.

The Sioux began collective cattle rearing to take the place of the lost bison hunt, but after further legislation invalidated treaty restrictions, the best grazing land and the water rights ended up in the hands of outsiders. Roxanne Dunbar Ortiz, a California State University sociologist, describes this tragedy in her *Indians of the Americas* (1984). She calls the battle over water rights the greatest new threat to the Indians' future.

By 1912, the Oglala on the Pine Ridge reservation had built up a cattle herd of 40,000, but then allotment, which came late here, hit them. Four years later, 2.5 million acres had been divided up and collective enterprises became awkward. In 1917 a new Indian Bureau agent suggested they should raise wheat instead, "to help the war effort" (this was World War I). The Oglala responded, and rented the bulk of their land to outside wheat growers. By 1930 two-thirds of their holdings had passed out of their control. By 1985 Indian farmers and ranchers were using 1 percent of the land, and more than half was being used by non-Indians.

Local judges got into the game. There is a case on record where after the death of a Creek Indian, a judge appointed eight white guardians, all to be paid out of the estate of the dead man.

On the Osage Oklahoma reservation, oil was found. Presently the Osage nation was supposed to draw a yearly income of $20 million from the find. Within years, white middlemen had their hands on 90 percent of the money.

Citizenship was played with. Thousands of Indians who had served in the U.S. army during World War I had been made citizens, and before that many states had procedures to make Indians citizens of the state their reservation was in. There were even romantic ceremonies where an Indian warrior "shot his last arrow" (literally) and then put his hands on the handles of a plow to show he was willing to become a U.S. citizen. I find a sense of decency in such goings-on, of seeing people as human beings. But when finally in 1924 all Indians born within the borders of the United States were declared citizens, the law was as ambivalent as all our Indian "deals." It professed not to affect anyone's belonging to a tribe, but this was then turned inside out and used to show that Indians were still second-class citizens: their tribal membership supposedly proved that they were not true "free individuals," able to act for themselves. I was not surprised to find that the Iroquois, Hopi, Onondaga, and others refused to accept citizenship on these terms.

The Iroquois showed their feelings about it when in 1942 they separately and independently declared war on Germany and the other Axis powers on behalf of their Confederation. (Many of them went on to serve in World War II.) In recent years, an Onondaga team of lacrosse players, returning from an international tour, refused to identify themselves at Kennedy Airport in New York City with anything but their Onondaga passports. They were kept waiting in a transit room for a day while frantic telephone conversations were made with Washington. They won: they were allowed to enter the country. Some Washington official must have realized that closing the border to the first Americans would give the government an international black eye. There is nothing childish about such Indian maneuvers: precedent is all.

By the late 1920s the corruption and the corrupters surrounding the Indians could no longer be ignored in Washington. The Secretary of the Interior asked for an independent report. Published in 1928, it showed that another half-century "of dishonor" had been added to the first. Housing, schools, health services, were all equally shoddy. Suicide rates and alcoholism (another form of suicide) were appalling. Congress had not

In June 1942, leaders of the Six Iroquois Nations came to Washington carrying a declaration of war on the Axis powers (Germany, Italy, and Japan), which were at war with the United States. The resolution was ratified in tribal meetings during the following month. [AP/Wide World Photos]

understood the strength found in tribal ownership. The Dawes Act had left the Indians even more in need of federal help than before; it had only benefitted "racketeers and land speculators."

THE JOHN COLLIER YEARS AND AFTER

As long as the mood of the nation at large did not change, there was little hope of change for the Indians. How could that mood change? The country had started this modern century of ours with a president, Teddy Roosevelt, who had once declared, "I don't go so far as to think that the only good Indians are dead Indians. But I believe nine out of ten are, and I shouldn't like to inquire too closely into the case of the tenth."

But when, in 1933, in the middle of the Great Depression, a different Roosevelt became president, the mood had changed greatly. Franklin Roosevelt appointed John Collier as the new Commissioner of Indian Affairs, and for the next twelve years the Indians too had a new deal.

There has been much criticism of Collier in recent Indian writing, and I am sure he was far from perfect. But then, no non-Indian could have been the perfect person to run Indian Affairs. Collier did bring in fresh air. Here was someone who admired Indian societies and who at least tried to understand them. He was the main author of the 1934 Indian Reorganization Act, the IRA, which replaced the Dawes mess. Under the IRA, land allotment was stopped and money was appropriated ($2 million a year) *to buy back* land for the Indians. A rotating loan fund was set up. Religious freedom was, finally, guaranteed for the Indians as it had long been for everyone else. Education was revamped. Above all, henceforth Indians were to participate in all planning affecting them. That's how it was written, but of course there would be a hundred little and big men who'd try to bend the new rules to their own interest.

Every Indian community was to vote on the IRA. One hundred and eighty-one tribes or nations accepted, but seventy-seven, including the largest, the Navajo, rejected it. This will only surprise you if you forget how many government officials they had seen come and go with their plans, promises, and tricks. Thus the IRA caused a split among native Americans, with "traditional" Indians opposing it and "progressives" supporting it. But the quotes around those two words are important. The realities of Indian history were not so clear-cut. There was much discussion among "traditionalists" who saw the IRA's strengthening

John Collier, Franklin Roosevelt's Commissioner of Indian Affairs, conferring with Seminole Indian leaders in Florida in 1940. [AP/Wide World Photos]

of tribalism as a possible trick meant to weaken Indian nationalism. At least, that is how I understand it. Yet the concept of one single Indian nation was remote, and many others saw tribal governments as a logical step toward one.

In retrospect it still seems to me that the IRA opened a door, if not a golden one. It did help move power away from the Washington bureaucracy to the mountains and plains. That, plus a new spirit of *respect* for things Indian instilled by Collier, indeed made for a new deal. The new funding, now, many years later, looks like small potatoes, but during the depression years it was a lot. Collier and Roosevelt at least put the money where their mouths were.

In 1948 the Bureau of Indian Affairs listed 10,000 new reservation families who had become rehabilitated and were self-supporting; 4 million acres added to the Indian land base; $12 million loaned for Indian enterprises, of which less than $4,000 had not been paid back: the best credit risk in America. Still it would all turn sour.

Roosevelt had died in 1945 and a new congressional mood was all for dismantling the New Deal. Collier was sent packing; he was "too leftish." A new cycle began. It is hard to believe, but Congress once again got high on assimilation, as a right this time, a "long-deserved right." It was now called "termination" but smelled as bad as under any other name: it meant, once more, distribution of the spoils, get the Indians off the federal budget.

Between 1954 and 1960, Congress in its sublime ignorance "terminated" a large number of Indian tribes and nations, divided tribal assets among the members, and sent the individual Indians into the true modern wilderness, the wilderness of cities. In the mid-1950s, life expectancy for a white man in Minneapolis, Minnesota, was sixty-eight years. For an Indian in the state of Minnesota it was forty-six years. For an Indian in the city of Minneapolis, it was thirty-seven years. Thirty-seven years, as in Europe during the Middle Ages!

WASHINGTON'S SOUND AND FURY, SIGNIFYING LITTLE

By this time, Washington was equivocating. The government wanted the Indians off the budget, yet the awful realities of Indian life forced it in the opposite direction. The U.S. Public Health Service just *had* to help them. The federal postwar school programs just had to include Indian schools. President Johnson's War on Poverty and his civil rights programs took in the Indians. All this was, as with citizenship, double-edged. The built-in, total individualism of the Civil Rights Act could easily undermine a tribal society. In the words of Ward Churchill (a Creek/Cherokee Metis), "They wanted to give us just enough sovereignty to sell our land to them and just not enough to say No to their offers." The last acts of war in the Conquest were (and still are) being waged by lawyers waving contracts and checks.

"Termination" ended as suddenly as it had begun. It was not formally withdrawn until 1970 when President Richard Nixon (of all people) sent a message to Congress that termination was "morally and legally unacceptable." Then in 1975 the Indian Self-Determination Act came along.... I am sorry, this gets repetitive. (Think how the average Indian must feel about it.) But, at last, it is not a bloody tale any more. The 1975 act specified the right of the tribes to have the final word on any Indian program. It gave them a veto on putting Indian children in white boarding schools (finally). It was not all that different from what Collier had proposed forty years earlier, but maybe this time it was for keeps. All progress is two steps forward, one step back (at best). The struggle continues or, as they say south of the border, *la lucha continua*.

In *The Road*, a bitter indictment of U.S. policies by two Indian writers (it's in the bibliography), it is pointed out that these Washingtonian cycles, first this, then that, then this again, are ruled by money: the Allotment Act came precisely, and not by coincidence, at the peak of homesteading, the settling of white immigrants on free land. The Indian Reorganization Act, with its program of buying back land, came in the middle of the Depression, when American farmland had reached its lowest price in a century.

In the cold and neutral light of statistics, this is without any doubt precisely true. But if it is meant to show that there is *nothing* but cynical self-interest in all these federal to's and fro's, it is an oversimplification. A number of politicians and public figures in recent years, and among them several of Indian descent, have meant well and done rather well. At times the best laid plans of these men and women have gone awry because among the Indian nations there is, naturally, no unanimity about the way ahead.

Hidatsa Indian leader George Gillette crying at the 1950 signing of a contract that turned over 155,000 acres to the U.S. government. The tribal lands were flooded when the Garrison Dam was built. [AP/Wide World Photos]

INDEPENDENCE AND ITS THORNS

The thorn hidden in the idea of Indian independence (one of the thorns) is that those nations cannot yet aim for true independence. They need the federal government, they need protection against the vultures, and they need support in hard cash.

Various congressmen, lumber company and mining executives, water-board presidents, and so on, have started telling us that "in the United States no individual or group possesses special rights." That statement is ignorant, dishonest, or both. The "special rights" of the Indian nations are no deluxe welfare handouts but *mortgage payments* (pathetically small mortgage payments) that the United States undertook to make for the 3 million square miles that it negotiated, stole, or conquered away from its original owners. They are treaty obligations and moral obligations stemming from the days when the United States deprived the Indians of the economic bases on which they had built their lives—lives of a better quality than any they have since been offered. During the Conquest, the United States did not give the Indians any rights; on the contrary: the Indians gave the United States certain rights.

The fishing rights and the water rights and the mineral rights of the Indian nations are as little "special rights" as the occupancy of a large mansion by a millionaire is a "special right." There is nothing "special" in the capitalist, free enterprise United States for some people to have a lot of something and others to have little, even if for once those others who have a lot (of fish, or of uranium, for instance) happen to be Indians. If the miserably barren land that the Indians had to accept for their lush holdings now turns out to be rich in oil or uranium, it should gladden our hearts that sometimes there is justice under the sky and that the race is not always to the swift.

AT LAST, ANGER?

An African-American woman recently asked me, "Why aren't Indians angry?" Many are. They are not people who wear their feelings on their sleeves. I think, though, that we must accept that after all these years "disgust" may describe their mood more accurately. In 1969, when change was in the air, a group of young people from different Indian nations occupied Alcatraz, the evacuated prison island in San Francisco Bay. Perhaps this wasn't even anger, but a simple act of self-assertion. In 1973, members of AIM, the American Indian Movement, occupied the massacre site of Wounded Knee to heal that long-festering trauma. You might have thought that the federal government would have been glad both times, glad that it was offered such simple and cheap ways for healing some of those old wounds. But no, Washington chose these occasions to appear in a holier-than-thou light, astounded that there exist people who do things not quite according to a rule book that Washington itself so often leaves closed.

When AIM tried to end years and years of Indian apathy and despondency, you might have thought that our government would have been glad and done its best to accommodate this new pride and energy. No such luck. It sent the FBI in by the dozens, those same fellows who were sure that students, then African-Americans, were going to blow up the country, and who now announced that the Indians were ready to do so; and who then did their best to bog down this new Indian energy and hope in a morass of provocation, arrests, and other legal harassment. None the less, AIM is still alive and kicking.

The Reagan-Bush years, with their philosophy of leaving Big Business alone to do its best and worst, and with their cuts in services, were as cold for native Americans as for all other Americans below the riches line. Reagan really had nothing to say but, "Bring in private enterprise and shoot for Indian capitalism." Some Indian groups had already been acting along these lines. Twenty-five western tribes had formed a council on the model of OPEC, the powerful voice of the big oil-producing countries. Indian nations were building casinos and race tracks for the tourist trade, as they are outside state jurisdiction for such undertakings. There aren't too many illusions about this: it isn't great but it's better than unemployment as long as you can keep the mafia out. What is wrong with it, in the words of law professor Rob Williams, himself an Indian, is this: as little as the Indian could and should have been forced into the role of a Yankee yeoman farmer, as little is it his or her destiny to become a yuppie entrepreneur.

The field of law was frozen too; tribes that were "terminated" on the sly in the 1950s are still waiting to have their rights restored (the Menominee managed to, in 1973). Tribes that missed out

Indians who have occupied the bare rock of Alcatraz (former federal prison in San Francisco Bay) vote on, and refuse, a federal government offer to turn the island into a national park. The year is 1970. [AP/Wide World Photos]

on treaty rights and have only what is still, unpleasantly, called "aboriginal title," are much overdue for a legal security that is not at the mercy of congressional moods. The Reagan-Bush Supreme Court appointees did not help either; "conservatism" here meant, not return to the constitution as John Marshall had seen it but a sterility that was by its nature hostile to Indian thought. Thus Supreme Court Justice Antonin Scalia wrote the majority decision in the 1991 "peyote case," which badly weakened the long-awaited American Indian Religious Freedom Act of 1978. (The peyote cactus, containing a hallucinogenic liquid, plays a role in certain Indian ceremonies.) Only Congress can now undo this damage.

After the all-time low of the year 1900, there are now some 2 million Indians living within the borders of the United States. There is no precise definition of the term "Indian": this is the number of people who declared themselves Indian in the 1990 census. Part of the rise may simply be due to more men and women being willing and able to do so than in the atmosphere of debilitating discrimination of earlier years. Many of them are not full-blooded Indians.

Thirty-one states of this country have trust lands or reservations, and in those states live some 1.8 million Indians, not necessarily on tribal land but usually with some ties to it. About 200,000 native Americans live on territory that now falls within the other nineteen states and the federal district.

Montana, North and South Dakota, and Oklahoma have the largest Indian land holdings, plus of course Alaska, where some nations are kin to the Apaches, some to the Inuit of Canada. Colorado's Democratic Senator Ben Nighthorse Campbell, elected in 1992, was the first native American in the Senate in seventy years. In New England, 30,000 declared themselves Indian in the 1990 census.

Against all odds, tribes and nations have survived, and have held together precisely because they have rejected the American ideology for themselves, both in its aspirations and in its dog-eat-dog competitiveness. Only thus have Indians remained Indians.

9

IN OUR BACK YARD

Latin Americans hate it when U.S. politicians talk about their countries as "our back yard," and you can see why. It's arrogant, and it's usually in a context where those politicians announce that "we" won't tolerate this, that, or the other. Turning it around, Latin America is indeed our back yard, which makes it the more shameful that it is in such a shocking state. Whenever leaders of integrity appeared on the Latin American scene, trying to better the miserable lives of the Indian peasants, they were as a rule quickly waylaid by the United States or by U.S. "interests" nervous about losing the privileges they had acquired. The big U.S. corporations never let the Latin Americans help their poor with such things as land reform and nationalization of their resources. Life was a lot better for a kid growing up in Warsaw than in São Paulo.

As I am writing this (early in 1993), things are less horrendous than they have recently been. That is to say, the wholesale slaughter of native populations by military governments has abated (but not ended). The recent history of some of these countries reads like so many lessons in morality: evil (even if it's supposed to be evil to avoid a worse evil), always breeds more evil. When, in 1950, Jacobo Arbenz Guzmán was elected president of Guatemala, the Mayan Indians got their first chance at a more decent life since 1524. That chance did not last long. President Eisenhower let the CIA arrange the 1954 overthrow of Arbenz Guzmán, as you can read in Ike's memoirs. Ever since, the military has ruled. Between 1970 and 1985, 100,000 civilians were murdered by their own government, and 40,000 people were disappeared (that is not a mistake in my grammar). Those are figures from the Organization of American States. Che Guevara was in Guatemala in 1954, and what happened there turned him into a revolutionary. How could Ike do this? How was it possible that a decent man who had fought the Nazis and seen their death camps was ready to condemn so many people to generations of death and suffering? Arbenz Guzmán was a leftist with a land-reform program and he had started nationalizing the large estates, many of which were lying fallow. He had started to give land back to Indian peasants after 430 years ... land including that of the United Fruit Company. But I don't suggest Ike was doing this for the sake of the profits of United Fruit. He saw it as another move in the global chess game with the Russians. For, obviously, natives don't know what's good for them: those Indians must have been put up to voting for Arbenz Guzmán by Russian agents running through their fields in dark hats and raincoats. I presume that in the unconscious recesses of President Eisenhower's mind, though, Guatemalan Indians weren't *really* men, women, and children. And Ike's recipe has since been tried again and again. In the Dominican Republic, Juan Bosch was gotten rid of; in Chile, Salvador Allende; in Brazil, João Goulart. Those men had been freely elected. They were progressives.

The recipe doesn't work out, not even if you check it on a non-moral scale that does not count suffering but only dollars.

At the entrance to the cathedral of Guatemala City in 1985, people are studying the names of Guatemalans who have disappeared. The right-wing government of Guatemala and its army murdered thousands of Indians, while more than 200,000—in a nation of less than 10 million—fled the country. [Olivia Huessler, Impact Visuals]

The cost to the United States of the upheavals, the training and putting in place of mercenaries and torturers, the refugees ending up at our borders, the loss in trade, the bad debts—it all adds up to many times the gain to "our" businesses and corporations.

All this is part of the story of the Conquest, for the basic disease of most of Latin America is not scarcity of resources, or even U.S. intervention. The disease is that the Conquest is not over. Millions of Indians are still fighting it. Those who aren't in the actual fight are like prisoners-of-war, caught behind walls of misery and contempt. But now it is rarely a fight over territory (except in Brazil's Amazon). And more and more it is not an armed struggle but a political fight for elementary civil rights, yet that does not mean that there is not an abundance of violence.

It is a complicated picture. Men and women of all races, liberals and socialists, ex-communists and still-communists, are jointly fighting for social justice and human rights against the traditional tyrants and bosses. In these fights, they used to take little account of the Indians fighting their own battle for autonomy or for the minimum needs of human life; but that is changing. Thus in Guatemala, in the last few years, the Maya Quiché and other Indian tribes have been given their due as valued allies, especially since the momentous award of the Nobel peace prize, in 1992, to a Maya Quiché woman, peasant leader and long-time exile Rigoberta Menchu. (I hope that this will help break the virtual blackout our media maintain on government violence. Early in 1993, the Guatemalan army bombed Indian rebel villages on the south coast of the country and in the Petén area. How many people here knew this?) In Nicaragua, the successful Sandinista revolution took its time to recognize the Miskito, Sumu, and other Indian tribes as fellow revolutionaries, but the Indians were on the road to autonomy when Violeta de Chamorro defeated the Sandinista Daniel Ortéga in the 1990 elections. The Indians have lost some momentum since, but it seems unthinkable that Chamorro would want to reverse their progress.

And in every other Latin American nation—with the exception of Argentina and Uruguay, which have a virtually white (European) population—Indian tribes find increasing recognition as indispensable allies if these nations are finally to shed the miserable inheritance of tyranny and exploitation left by the Conquest. Of course there is still racism, among the *mestizos* as well as among the *creoles,* but the contrasts and conflicts are often of class, of middle class against poor, and of town against countryside, rather than of race as such. And with the dying out of the Cold War fantasies, managers of vast estates and corporations are having to abandon the claim that they aren't exploiting the poor but are saving their countries from "Soviet Communism."

The battle map changes day by day. As I write this, the most bitter result of the Conquest is being played out in Peru. Here descendants of the Incas have, after centuries of mute despair, broken out in the rage of the *Sendero Luminoso,* the "Shining Path." Are we surprised? Did those twentieth-century ladies and gentlemen *conquistadores,* strolling through the shopping streets of Lima and carefully stepping over the starving Quechua Indians in the doorways, think this would go on forever and ever? The violence of *Sendero* may be self-defeating, but in judging it we must realize that it is the mirror rage of the very violence perpetrated on the Indians from Pizarro onward.

In Brazil, violence originates, as it has through centuries, with the other side, the oppressors. Here settlers can still buy "clean land," land from which armed gangs have chased the original population, if not killed them. But here too, as in Central America and Ecuador and Bolivia, the Indians are fighting back. They are not alone either, as Chico Mendes, the (*mestizo*) Indian union leader who was an organizer in their fight, proved—until he was murdered by what the press called the "loggers' interests." The Indians have a desperate battle ahead of them: in Brazil they have the "right of occupation" of their land and no more, as in the United States in the early days. The government grants mining concessions where it wants and does not seriously protect the Indians against miners, ranchers, and looters. At the same time, there is a proposed law that would "emancipate" them (not unlike the "termination policy" in the United States), and in the process deprive them of the bit of protection their tribal status now gives them. In 1986 (the most recent figures), 537 mining claims had been given out in "reserved" indigenous areas. The list of Indian tribes pushed aside or decimated through hydro-electric projects, roads, and armed prospectors names seventeen different tribal groups.

These horrors do not take place only in hidden wildernesses. The uprooted Indians, refugees in their own land, flock to the cities. The statistics tell us that half the Indian children of São

Paulo in 1993 do not live to see their tenth birthday. Brazil is not a pauper country, there is wealth there, the Sunday papers have two hundred pages and are printed in six colors; São Paulo is the largest city, with 17 million inhabitants. I have seen the São Paulo slums. It was a sight so horrendous that I felt I could not stay; I left the same evening. I sat in a taxi, a little Volkswagen Beetle; there had been a long line of those at the bus station where I arrived. I asked the Indian driver where he lived. "Are you joking?" he asked. "Here. We live right here." They slept in their taxis. That driver owned *nothing* except another shirt.

The brightest light in this dark landscape may be international solidarity. A key date was 1977, when the Indians forced the world to take notice of their fight: that was the year of the first international conference of the indigenous peoples of the Americas, held at the United Nations Center for Human Rights in Geneva, Switzerland. A hundred Indian representatives from the Americas attended. Ever since, the United Nations has played an increasing role in the struggle and indeed, if the UN has a brief in Iraq and Bosnia, it surely has a brief here too. A seat in the UN General Assembly for a representative of the indigenous nations is one of their goals. And, luckily, the 1992 Quincentennial debate has greatly helped the Indians in their struggle. What began as a "celebration" of Columbus' landfall backfired and led to a new public awareness of the realities of the Conquest. Thousands of Indians in both North and South America became politicized and drawn into the fight for true emancipation.

As told earlier, in Mexico the battle lines are somewhat different. Here the Conquest was fought to a standstill by the *mestizos* and Indians. They elected their own president, Benito Juárez, a Zapotec Indian, in 1858—337 years after the fall of Tenochtitlán. But such battles are not won that easily. The fight had to be taken up once more early in this century, to overthrow that tenacious *conquistador* Porfirio Díaz, who with his followers ruled and plundered Mexico for thirty-four years, until 1911. The foot soldiers in that drawn-out revolutionary war were also Indians, humble men who moved from battle to battle across the vast, roadless country in freight trains, accompanied by their wives or girlfriends who fought at their sides and fed them and nursed them, the *soldaderas*, true heroines of those years. When Emiliano Zapata led his troops into Mexico City, the citizens locked themselves in their houses, but the Zapatistas were not the rapists the Díaz press had announced; they were Indian peasants who shuffled down the streets, clutching their pesos to buy something to eat. They were photographed in the coffee shop of Mexico City's Sanborn department store buying breakfast; you see them with their rifles sticking out over the counter, staring solemnly at the waitresses, who stare back with equal solemnity. The year was 1914; these soldiers had liberated the capital. Most of them were doomed to perish. There is neither pride nor fear on their faces— some embarrassment perhaps. The Sanborn waitresses still wear the same uniforms as in that famous photo.

Zapata was betrayed; much of the fighting was in vain. But eventually the tide turned once more and in 1934 that country got a president with the power and integrity to lead a "peaceful democratic revolution." He was Lázaro Cárdenas, contemporary of our Franklin Roosevelt. His six-year term led to a drastic change in landownership: the number of peasants working their own land grew from less than 10 percent to 50 percent. The economic impact of this was disappointing and Mexico's poor remained poor; but a new consciousness of dignity among the Indians as a result of the Cárdenas years has lasted. In 1940, there was a reaction to the Cárdenas populism, and a string of conservative presidents followed each other, as political power became the monopoly of one party, which soon was revolutionary in name only. Now the progressive opposition in Mexico is stronger than it has ever been in the last half-century. With pleasing historical symmetry, it is led by Lázaro Cárdenas' son. There is a general feeling in the country that it is only a matter of time before the entrenched political machine is defeated by this son, whose first name, most appropriately, is Cuauhtemoc (pronounced

Kevatémoc). This leader of the opposition was named after the last free Aztec, hanged by Cortés; his victory will be an Indian victory.

Paraguay has hardly any inhabitant without Guaraní Indian blood and in Paraguay you hear more Guaraní spoken than Spanish. Sadly, this doesn't mean that the native population has any political power. To the contrary, during the endless locust years of their dictator General Alfredo Stroessner (he had a neon advertisement in the capital saying, "Stroessner—Bread—Work—Freedom") they lost more land than ever before, and now almost three-quarters of the local Indians have no land at all and work as laborers on the farms of the large landowners. Stroessner was finally kicked out in 1989 but not much has changed so far. U.S. military aid is quite visible; everywhere you see the peasant army conscripts, small, undernourished, Guaraní and Chaco Indians, their somber faces half hidden under those big bucket U.S. helmets—a depressing sight.

Cuba—ah, Cuba. Here racism was really rooted out, out of the public and official life of the country, that is. (No one but its owner can root it out of the heart.) Three thousand Jamaicans in London, British citizens, would yearly apply for a visa at the Cuban embassy there, one of the less published emigration queues of our time. Few would be let in; there was no housing. Cuba blew a breath of fresh air into poor, struggling, Latin America in that exhilarating January of 1959 when Fidel Castro and Che Guevara drove into Havana with their campesinos, and Batista and his U.S. gangsters fled the country. Centuries of injustice had to be undone; before Batista there had been the U.S. marines and the mafia, before them the Spanish and British "sugarocracy" which had burned down the woods, evicted the small farmers, and turned the island into a huge slave-run sug-armill. (Brazil and Cuba had been the last great slave centers of the world until the last decades of the nineteenth century; Cuba under Spain, Brazil "independent.") Here the book of the Conquest was finally closed.

But Castro was squeezed ever harder by the blockade and the hostility of the United States and he had nowhere to turn but to the Soviet Union. When they stopped their aid, Cuba became a poor country again, with little political freedom but still with free education, free medical care, a flourishing theater and arts, and racial equality. The drama is not over, but it would be a bad day for this hemisphere if the United States were seen to have smothered this great venture.

It is precisely the *fear*, the guilty fear of the rich in Latin America of their own people, that has opened the doors again and again to those slick colonels and captains, those men with their rows of campaign ribbons earned by killing their own peasants. A fear fed by contempt, a contempt fed by fear. In a word: racism.

I have been astounded by the hatred that nice tea-drinking ladies showed for their own compatriots. This was in Argentina, a country where most of the free Indians have been exterminated and where the peasants show a feudal humility. It was a racism of class. They were scared of their own poor, right in the heart of Buenos Aires, whose telephone directory lists some forty pages of military establishments.

You have to take that into account when drawing a balance of U.S. policies. The guilt is not all ours. For every U.S. marine landing in Latin America, there were and are local Latin Americans only too glad to be protected by U.S. weaponry from their own exploited and disinherited.

10

FIVE HUNDRED YEARS

The Indians of the United States are the survivors, and the descendants of survivors, of an enormous crime. We live in a land where the number of Indians was reduced by 90 percent, where life for nine out of ten Indians was made unlivable. One of the many ways in which this was done called for the slaughter of the 80 million American buffalo. The Indian nations are the survivors of a manmade disaster. And we have learned from plane wrecks and hurricanes that disaster survivors need help. They need money, but not just money. We here in the United States cannot sit still and wait until general goodwill and human kindness start flowing down our streets; it is up to the government, *now,* to give the Indians the time and the room to shape their own destinies once more. This is certainly not the time for clever congressmen to start proving that federal parkland must "never" be used to help Indians, and it is not the time for smart lawyers to try and turn old Indian treaties and agreements "quite legally" against the Indian.

PRESENT DANGERS

Precisely because most reservations are outside state jurisdiction, do waste-disposal enterprises and nuclear-waste lawyers think they have found a ready-made victim role for the Indian tribes. It is hard for people living in the desolation of most of these places, where unemployment often runs to 60 percent, to refuse offers of such as the one made by the O & G Corporation of Connecticut, which wants to buy space for a 5,000-acre dump on the Rosebud Lakota reservation. It's a measure of the degree to which our government has failed in its job of trustee that instead of protecting the Indians against such Pied Pipers, it acts as their agents. The U.S. Department of Energy has approached every single reservation with offers for cash in return for storage space for nuclear waste. They have a spokesperson who went on record with this statement: "Because of the Indians' great care and regard for nature's resources, Indians are the logical people to care for the nuclear waste. Radioactive materials have a half-life of thousands of years.... It is the native American culture and perspective that is best designed to correctly consider and balance the benefits and the burdens."

Can you believe it? The same people who built nuclear reactors, and never mind the consequences, who told us that a bit of radioactivity and a bit of carcinogens won't hurt you, are now telling the Indians that because they look at nature in a different way, they should become the recipients of our poisonous excreta.

Then there's water. Land without water is useless, and hydro-electric dams, factory contamination, irrigation water stolen from their streams by agriculture and by towns, are all turning reservations into deserts. And so half-hearted, again, is the federal protection that the Indians have to go to court whenever some new enterprise or city council or water board has thought of a

A 1992 Columbus Day demonstration outside the United Nations in New York City demanding a seat in the UN General Assembly for a representative of the indigenous nations. [Kirk Condyles, Impact Visuals]

clever way to swindle them out of their water. At any one time, a hundred or more major lawsuits are in the works, in which Indians try to ward off these robbers. Years go by, the robbery goes on, appeal follows appeal, the Indians get poorer, the lawyers get richer.

Thus the mortal threat to the Crees of eastern Canada, whose land would be turned into lakes or stony deserts by the dam building of Hydro-Québec, a project, it so happens, that we in the United States can stop if we refuse to buy its electricity. The Crees live in one of the last pieces of "unsubdued" nature.

Whatever is left of unsubdued nature on this continent is as a rule inhabited by Indians. They have become the trustees of our wilderness.

Another inroad is made by industries that seduce reservations into building factories free of charge, with free Indian trainee labor, and which pull out when the gravy has been ladled off, that is, when the time has come to make such factories into ordinary market-price operations. Roxanne Dunbar Ortiz documents a case in detail, the story of Fairchild Semiconductor, which in 1969 acquired such a free plant on a Navajo reservation. In 1974 Fairchild started replacing union-member Indians with whites and the Navajo workforce staged a sit-in. The federal government tried to negotiate a settlement, but Fairchild simply moved its plant to Taiwan. Ortiz documents that, contrary to the story at the time, the Indian workers were as productive as the white ones and that they had less absenteeism. (Fairchild has since been sold to National Semiconductors, which didn't answer a request of mine for their comments.)

The Indians are not, as are other minorities, a group who could make it if their individual rights were protected. They are of and with the land; they need an iron-clad Magna Carta for Land.

(In the meantime, there's one thing that will not cost a penny: let the government, and the law, stop calling Indian lands "reservations," with its deadly connotation of "concentration camp." The Canadian term "reserves" is better, but not much better. Those areas are the last redoubts of our Indian nations— "the first nations," as they call themselves in Canada.)

THE INDIANS OF CANADA

In Canada it all happened later. Indians were valued as guides, as allies in war, as fur traders. Then the land grab began there too, and the government put a Victorian policy in place of one part paternalism, one part sentiment, and one part ruthlessness. It made for a poisonous pudding which overnight made the Indians

Empty barrels abandoned by the Canadian army on Cree land in Canada. [Kirk Condyles, Impact Visuals]

prisoners in their own country, and which saw to it that a man such as Louis Riel was hanged for "high treason." Riel had founded a *metis* (mixed blood) republic in Saskatchewan in 1885. There is now a building in downtown Winnipeg named after him. A meager consolation.

All in all it was the same dreary story, if in a slightly less bloody version. Canada had a "Great Mother," i.e., Queen Victoria, instead of a "White Father," i.e., the President in Washington, to put a signature on the various treaties and agreements. At the turn of the century, Canada's Indians counted 100,000 survivors, perhaps one-fifth, perhaps less, of the population when the Europeans came. But now their number is back up to over half a million.

Canada has since also had a go at "termination," but it only lasted two years, and its first nations are doing better than the

Indian nations of the United States in the battle for sovereignty. In 1990, one single Indian representative in parliament managed to kill the Meech Lake agreement, which spelled out Québec's sovereignty but did not mention any other minorities.

The Inuit (Eskimos) of the eastern Arctic are doing best in this long fight, but then they have a very powerful ally in their ice and snow. They are on the verge of assuming full jurisdiction over a new nation, Nunavut, which will be the largest land area under native American rule and will run from the northern border of Manitoba all the way to the North Pole.

On a bleak Sunday afternoon in November, I set foot on a Canadian reserve for the first time. It was part of the Sagkung First Nation, of the Ojibwa Indians, an hour's drive north of Winnipeg on a lake shore. For the last ten miles we followed a one-lane road, for the Indians refused to have it widened on their territory.

November in Manitoba is not a cheerful month, but in the flat, snowy landscape under a whitish winter sky, the reserve still came as a shock of more intense somberness. Small houses were scattered over a barren plain. Just beyond the border of the reserve stood a papermill, belching smoke and polluting a river and, through the river, the lake. Not a soul was in sight.

My companion, an Ojibwa who edits the reserve's bimonthly newspaper, told me they had regained the hunting rights in the adjacent woods, straight up to the Hudson Bay. But they only hunted for their own meat, and at times for an animal skin to sell in Winnipeg. He talked with great bitterness of the papermill. There were no jobs on the reserve; this fragment-of-a-nation was really but a camp for people dependent on government subsidies. The roads were unpaved, they had no shops, nothing. A forlorn dog. Snow. Wind.

"We used to have horses," the editor said. "We need people to come and tell us about that. It's a lost skill among us, taking care of them. It is a possibility." We went into the children's center, where a woman alone was on duty at the phone. The usual call was from a house where a parent—often the mother—had passed out from drink and the children needed help. It was around two in the afternoon and she had already dealt with nine such calls that day.

We walked through the deep snow to the lake shore. Here they were trying to create a little beach that would bring summer visitors from Winnipeg. A stretch had been cleared of undergrowth, and two signs had been put up with rules for bathers. That was all so far. The pollution of the lake was invisible under the snow-covered ice, and it was a beautiful setting. I asked the editor if people from the reserve, especially children, sailed or rowed on the lake in summer. The question surprised him. "No, no one," he said. "We have no boats. Such things are not in our customs."

It was a forlorn feeling, standing there in this white infinity. It was already getting dark and there wasn't a light visible anywhere. Perhaps if you had been born there, you'd feel at home. But it would never be like the feeling of a Cree or Ojibwa *who knew no other place.*

THE CONQUEST OF HAWAII

As it is now a part of the United States and thus a part of America, Hawaii has to be included in the Conquest story. The native Hawaiians are Polynesians. Captain Cook estimated the inhabitants at 400,000. That was in 1778. For 1900, the figure is 30,000, a minority in a population of 150,000, mostly foreign-born nationals, the majority Japanese. In 1898, the United States annexed the islands. In 1920, Congress set aside 200,000 acres to be homesteaded by those men and women whose ancestry was at least 50 percent Hawaiian. There are now 50,000 such people, but for mysterious reasons only 6,000 got land over the past seventy years, and more than 20,000 remain on the waiting lists. The New York Center for Constitutional Rights has taken their case.

Until 1893, Hawaii was a recognized independent kingdom. That didn't stop a U.S. missionary from announcing (the year was 1864) that the dying out of its people could be compared to "the amputation of diseased members of a body." Here's one more image of the native American for our collection: "diseased member." It can join "wolf," "lice," "devil worshippers," and "red-crayon sketch of humanity, to be rubbed out." That last one is the most picturesque of all, but then it came from a poet, Oliver Wendell Holmes, the father of a Supreme Court judge and himself a Doctor of Laws of Harvard and Oxford.

THE BETRAYAL BY ACADEMIA

I have written earlier about the failure of the United States schoolbooks to paint an honest picture of the American past. Now, in the 1990s, many books try to avoid controversy: when they deal with Columbus, they end the account after the first voyage, before the Conquest got down to business. They avoid the word "discovery" and speak of "encounter." "Encounter," though, is a mild word for an event where one group invaded the lands of another and virtually finished them off.

What are they afraid of? Isn't controversy in the classroom, with research and books and words, better than controversy in the streets with guns and knives? Racism, which may tear this multiracial country apart, can surely not be cured except by vying for the truth, a truth that will give all children, of all colors, a sense of perspective, a sense of dignity.

The bias and the omissions do not start with our schoolbooks. They start at the highest levels of academic wisdom. Many of our learned professors seem able to compartmentalize their minds. They know the facts, of course, but they manage not to let these disturb their self-satisfaction. They seem to tell themselves, at some inaudible dog-whistle pitch, that in the end it was still all really for the best.

Lewis Hanke, a Philadelphia professor, wrote a book (around 1950) about the soul-searching that went on in sixteenth-century Spain while the *conquistadores* were doing their worst. He called it *The Spanish Struggle for Justice in the Conquest of America.* Think a moment about that title. Whom were they struggling with? With themselves, presumably; the Indians weren't trying to keep them from practicing justice. But it must have been a struggle with words only; nothing emerged from it but edicts such as that the Indians should be sent to the mines "as nearly as possible with their consent." Who is Hanke kidding when he suggests that "justice" was the issue? Did he never wonder, during all the research that produced his avalanche of dates and names, whether justice and conquest can go together?

Read this passage from another famous book, Carl Sauer's *The Early Spanish Main,* published by the University of California Press: "Ovando [a successor to Columbus] made the island Hispaniola an attractive and profitable enterprise. The administration was efficient and honest.... The success was attained by breaking down the native social structure and subjecting the natives to excessive forced labor. The attrition of the native population was so great that other islands began to be raided to provide laborers."

Science must keep its cool, without emotion, and Sauer succeeds there. But now note the words "attractive" and "honest." Don't they have an emotional content? Note the impersonal "other islands began to be raided," instead of "Spanish slavers began to raid other islands." Note the word "attrition" for mass deaths and the word "laborers" for the slaves.

There is a new crop of more enlightened writers on the scene, as my bibliography shows, but I did not have to hunt for the passages quoted above. Hanke and Sauer are still established authorities, and many other historians still write in that same vein. Many, if not most, teachers in our junior high and high schools read these books in their college days.

What we teach in our schools and what we are taught as students is crucial as to how we behave in life. A real push forward and a real chance for American Indians to partake in that famous pursuit of happiness—if perhaps not a happiness as they once had—must come from a new perspective in this country. The real stumbling block is, still, the hostility of their non-Indian neighbors. Too many of these still imagine that equality means conformity to some undefined "way of life." It is astounding that the vast majority still feels threatened by that 1 percent Indian minority, that it sees as outsiders those who, in the true light of history, are the only insiders. And more astounding, so many Americans still manage to be *jealous* of the few crumbs the Conquest has left the Indian nations, the few salmon-streams, the strips of free land. Do they really want to behave like robbers who come back again and again, through the years, to make sure that their victims have nothing of value left?

GUILT AND THE WHITE RACE

If the Moorish armies had beaten Charles Martel in the battle of Poitiers, France, in 732 and had gone on from there to conquer the rest of Europe, "Blacks and Whites together" (as the civil rights song said) might now be brothers and sisters and Harlem might be a truly integrated black-and-white ghetto, trying to grasp some power from the Moorish rulers in Manhattan and Washington. But the Arabs lost that one. And while there is no merit in losing battles, it thus happened that it is the Europeans and their descendants who are still sitting pretty on all that loot and on the mountain of skulls. It was the looting of America that paid for the Industrial Revolution. It was the sweat and blood of unnamed generations of slaves that put Europeans in real houses, with regular meals on the table and shoes on their feet, that freed them from the traditional economy of scarcity and that made them, and their outposts, the masters of the world.

Of course, "Europeans" stand here for the upper classes of those societies, those who held the power and the money, they and the leaders of the new middle class. During the heyday of the Conquest, the slums of Madrid and of London were as remorseless as the slums of São Paulo are now. Colonizing started at home; the Spaniards practiced on their own peasants and by exterminating the natives of the Canary Islands; the Portuguese on the Azores; the English learned the job in Ireland. All of Europe—and all other layer-cake class societies—had a "mystique of class" in which the poor were a different species. (Nor has that idea been overcome everywhere.) But as the lowly of those countries came to America, the mystique of class was handily turned into a mystique of race. That way, the lowly whites did not have to be given an equal share of the loot and yet they'd still do most of the fighting, and feel themselves members of one large and cozy family, the "white race."

Writing in this fashion of the "white race," of Europe, I am not underestimating the cruelty of peoples in other lands. Their conquests, too, make a horrible tale. Perhaps the Europeans had more persistence than most, were more inclined to stop at nothing. However that may be, I am dealing with America's Conquest, America's past. I am not gratuitously pointing at any one country. And I am not idealizing the pre-1492 nations of the Americas.

My own country of origin, Holland, rebelled against Spain in the sixteenth century and the king of Spain sent his most inhuman *conquistador,* the Duke of Alva, up north to subdue it. But when the Dutch had won that war, they started their voyages to the East Indies, where they took their turn to behave like *conquistadores.* The human race, humanity, had—and still has—a long way to go if it is to deserve the labels of "civilized" and "humane" which most of us are so ready to bestow upon ourselves. Historically speaking, I do not believe that a very different scenario for America over the past five hundred years could ever have been in the cards. But this does not eradicate the individual guilt of the settlers, men and women who were so very quick to see themselves as the bringers of "white civilization" to a "dark continent." It is high time then to reevaluate the heroes and heroines of the American past and the values they held, in theory and in actuality.

I am not talking of "liberal guilt complexes"—the guilt is only too real. On the other hand, I am surely not suggesting that the United States steep itself in a mud-bath of guilt. There are instances of such behavior in the past, and it is often followed by a backlash where evil gets back into its own and is equated with "political realism." This story is not out to create guilt or shame as private emotions, with a possible self-satisfied aftertaste of nobility. It is out to create guilt or just simply knowledge as a motive for action. "History is written by the victors," Hitler used to say. Let American children take pride then in being a first generation to break out of that vicious division between the children of the victorious and the children of the defeated. Let us begin studying and writing a history of winner and victims both. Let us show that much respect for the many dead. Here is a true glory, a true reason for being proud of one's country.

And because this is a new idea, the writers of such history must be very precise or they might provide ammunition for those who don't want to give up the comforts of racial arrogance and contempt. There are many stories and theories which may change our image of the long-ago past of this continent, such as the Mayans or Africans crossing the Atlantic ocean a thousand years ago; I have not mentioned them because there is no proof of them, not yet. The conquest, though, is a historical fact. The burden it places on all of us does not change character whether any of this did or did not happen.

Indians "see God in the clouds, or hear him in the wind." Alexander Pope, the English poet, wrote that (he considered it a sign of their ignorance). When I write about learning from the Indians, I think of learning to look at life that way. I am not suggesting that the Indian nations hold a secret that can give this country of 250 million people back its beauty and purity, such as it must have been in 1492. Europe, outside its pestilential cities, was also beautiful in 1492. We cannot undo the Industrial Rev-olution unless we are prepared to let nine-tenths of the world die of hunger. We can learn a different approach, a turning away from our obsessive more-more-more. We could even—without waiting for the unavoidable calamities that would teach us that lesson—learn that redistribution, *sharing* the world's wealth, is our only way ahead.

I guess it will be a miracle if we really get this straight. But it is also a miracle that the Indians are still in our midst and that their civilization still has the vitality to give a boost to that idea.

The United States is a multiracial society and will in the future be even more so—a society of people from all over the globe. We can only hope for harmony if we see this as positive, as a mirror of the beautiful variety of life. In this future, the role of the native Americans is of the essence.

Simon Bolívar said that we here are neither Europeans nor true Americans and that therefore we shall never be happy.

It is not beyond our power, though, to finally heal the wounds of the Conquest, and gainsay his prophesy.

A BIBLIOGRAPHY

In the beginning was Columbus; and in the beginning was Bartolomé de las Casas. His *Devastation of the Indies* is back in print in English translation, published by The Johns Hopkins University Press. It is just a little paperback and it remains the eye-opener it was on its publication 440 years ago. Also back in print is *The Four Voyages of Christopher Columbus,* a fine selection of source material from that time edited by John Michael Cohen and first published as a paperback by Penguin Books in 1969.

When I began work on my own Columbus book in 1975, I could not find one high-school or general text that didn't treat Columbus as the glorious hero he was not. Now, with the Quincentennial and its new awareness behind us, more serious books are beginning to appear. But most schoolbook or children's book writers (as I've mentioned) deal with this new approach by simply confining themselves to the first voyage. That way you get the adventure, Columbus' "first," and none of the tragedy that started when the Conquest started, which was with the second voyage. It's not honest, and thus I am not shy about mentioning my own *Columbus: His Enterprise,* which Monthly Review Press published in a new paperback in 1991, and which has also been translated into Spanish as *Colon, El Mito Al Descubierto* (published by Ed. de la Flor in Buenos Aires in 1992). The Spanish edition is readily available in the United States through Bilingual Publications in New York City.

In 1991 the Chicago Religious Task Force on Central America (don't let the long name scare you off) published a big workbook, mainly directed at teachers and students, with many illustrations, questions to be answered, and a wealth of references: it is called *DangerousMemories.* It starts with Columbus and carries on from there. Two more books about the early years are: G. R. Crone's *The Discovery of America* and Carl Ortwin Sauer's *The Early Spanish Main.* They were published in the 1960s and I am aggrieved by their basic point of view, as I explained earlier, but they are filled with fascinating facts and known for their learning. They're out of a print but a decent library will have them on its shelves.

I have mentioned the new work scholars have done on the size of the pre-1492 population of the Americas. They are called the "Berkeley school." Some of their books are: Henry Dobyns' *Their Number Became Thinned* (University of Tennessee Press, 1983), William Denevan's *The Native Population of the Americas in 1492* (University of Wisconsin Press, 1976), and (for Peru only), David Cook's *Demographic Collapse* (Cambridge, England, 1981). A fascinating book focussing on just one aspect of the Conquest is E. J. Hamilton's *American Treasure and the Price Revolution in Spain,* which shows how little good all the plunder did the plunderers; it was published in 1934 by Harvard University Press and is in print.

Richard Drinnon's *Facing West* (University of Minnesota Press, 1980) is a beautiful book about what lies behind it all: European attitudes toward the Indians and "natives" in general.

I have to thank Drinnon for some of the material in Chapter 7, above all the dog Dugdale whom I'll never forget. The most famous books along these lines are Eduardo Galeano's *Open Veins of Latin America,* first published by Monthly Review Press in 1973, and his *Memory of Fire* (Pantheon, 1985). They are a source for every student and writer on this subject.

Roxanne Dunbar Ortiz, the Californian sociologist, wrote *Indians of the Americas* (Praeger, 1984), the same title that Roosevelt's Commissioner of Indian Affairs John Collier had chosen for his book. Ortiz' work is original and important; her focus is on the legality and illegality of various "Indian policies," and on what native Americans may expect from international action. *The Road: Indian Tribes and Political Liberty,* by Russell Barch and James Youngblood Henderson (University of California Press, 1980) deals with the same subject. The most recent book from the Quincentennial crop, which I read and used, is David Stannard's *American Holocaust,* published by Oxford University Press in the fall of 1992. Stannard, a professor at the University of Hawaii, gives the numbers, and places, the where, and the how, to justify his title. The reception this book receives may give us a good indication of how ready we, and academia, are to face these facts.

Native American Testimony (Viking-Penguin, 1991), edited by Peter Nabokov, is a collection of what the Indians themselves have said through these fateful centuries. They should have the last word on the matter.

If you want to read about the ways of nineteenth-century Europeans in a more general framework, look at V. G. Kiernan's *The Lords of Human Kind,* written by a man with a great sense of humor. It was published by Weidenfeld in London in 1969 and is still in print. To study those ways in the raw, so to speak—that is, as expounded by people who took them for granted—just read at random in the eleventh edition of the *Encyclopaedia Britannica* (1910/1911), famous, and in many public libraries. To read up on U.S. history in general, seen from a more enlightened, or, if you will, from a less self-satisfied, point of view, Howard Zinn's *A People's History of the United States* (a paperback) is a fine book, breaking new ground. (As late as November 1992, a New York City school librarian refused to put it in a bibliography.)

The Quincentennial gave a great boost to native American studies, and many organizations and many new magazines are now making serious material available on all levels, from grade school to postgraduate. Here are some of them:

CALC (Clergy and Laity Concerned), 198 Broadway, New York City 10038, and P.O. Box 1987, Decatur, GA 30031.

AICH (American Indian Community House), 404 Lafayette Street, New York City 10003.

Rethinking Schools, 1001 E. Keefe Avenue, Milwaukee, WI 53212.

MRG (Minority Rights Group), a research group in London that publishes reports on many indigenous nations and groups. They are available in the United States from Cultural Survival, 53/A Church Street, Cambridge, MA 02138.

OXFAM, 274 Banbury Road, Oxford OX2 7OZ, England, which puts out "poster packs," very useful and bright, for grade school students.

CASNP (Canadian Alliance in Solidarity with Native Peoples), PO Box 574, Stn P, Toronto M5S 2T1, Canada, which publishes a thick catalog of native American sources and books for teachers and children, each one rated according to age and to point of view—a marvelous summing up, doing justice to native American authors and better than anything in the United States so far.

AN AFTERWORD FROM ALEXANDER EWEN

Alexander Ewen is a member of the Native American Council of New York. I want him to have the last word, and what follows are passages from a speech he made in the fall of 1992, when we both participated in a Columbus Teach-In organized by the New York City Learning Alliance. Alex is a member of the Purepecha Nation.

"I am not a fan of multiculturalism, but it is largely because I can't see how, if you cannot get one people's history right, you are possibly going to bring in another people's history and hope to get that right. Yet we value being able to talk to educators, and try to convince them of the need to inject other people's values and other people's thinking into Western culture....

"When we look at the rise of the environmental movement, we have to look for its roots. Part of it is in the majesty of the

American wilderness, certainly. A tremendous, beautiful land-scape cared for by native people. But part of it was also from people who knew Indians, sat down with people like Sitting Bull, and learned the importance of respecting the earth.

"Look at Greenpeace today and their model of the Rainbow Warrior. We know where it comes from. This is Indian thinking, the kind of thinking that native people were brought up with and that is now infusing itself into Western thought and influencing it tremendously. We need to find out more about those roots, because it tells us more about where we are going and where we want to be. It is not enough to look at the facts. The facts are terrible and as obvious as can be. The fact is that the height of European technology, what Europe could show the world, its pride and major achievement, was its ability to make war. And it continues to be that. The cutting edge of Western technology is destruction.

"And we could look at this hemisphere and say the pride of Indian technology, what it could show the people, were different things. Unless I got hit by a garbage truck, I'd prefer a medicine man. Ancient Indian agricultural technology holds its own with Western agricultural technology. Your average Indian in the Northeast could outproduce a Pilgrim by four to one. And the average Indian in the Northeast couldn't hold a candle to the Mayas and the Aztecs, who could produce huge, vibrant, popu-lous cities and support them in such a way that they sat in the middle of nature....

"Another gift was government. Sophisticated governments, that were highly developed, with balances of power, and which included women as decision makers.... Lastly, the prophecy, the areas of metaphysics that Western society has now thrown aside. It doesn't believe in metaphysics anymore. Only in science. It only believes that you have to see it, touch it, experiment with it, and prove it. It doesn't recognize that there are many things in this world you cannot do this to. It will not believe that there are things in this world that might actually be smarter than humans, and therefore are not going to allow themselves to be tested. It does not believe that the possibility exists that humans are upsetting a well-crafted order that has been in place for tens of thousands of years, and that a time can come when that order is upset so badly that there is no point of return.

"So we can look quickly at two different hemispheres and we can say, "What can you show for yourself?" But because of the lack of *discovery*, the lack of an attempt, any time, to try to learn what the people of this hemisphere had to say, we are missing— and not just from Indians, there are African and Asian people who have much to contribute to this world—we are missing the vast library that is the human race. We are only looking at a small, new, constantly-being-rewritten-to-suit-someone's-opinion book.

"As we look at the future, some things need to be made clear. Today, if we can take a step back to look at this hemisphere, we see that the last remaining stretches of wilderness are all in Indian hands, and controlled by native people. Whether it is the Amazon, northern Canada, the Arctic, the rainforests of Central America, they all belong to the Indians who live in them and form the first line of defense for these areas. This is the issue, the struggle, nothing else is important. Ethnically clean areas do not mean anything if there is an ozone hole that will wipe out life on earth. We need to change the path that Western culture has embarked on—quickly—and focus it on a whole different kind of thinking and learning.

"The first Western discipline we should abandon is the pseudoscience of economics. It is an ideology, not a science, based upon fundamental assumptions that are incorrect. Fifty years ago Will Rogers said, "If you lay all the economists in this country end to end, they will all point in different directions." A fundamental assumption of current economic theory is that things have value only in terms of money, and that things only have value when they are transformed into products for the market. Trees create value only by being cut down and used.

Another assumption is that ownership rights and property rights are scientific principles and that they are the best means to manage and protect land and institutions. Only if you own it, will you have an interest in protecting it, and if no one owns it, such as the ocean, or the sky, there is no incentive to protect it. The truth is that trees, oceans, people, children, have value other than what they produce or what they can be sold for. The assumptions that guide mainstream economics have nothing to do with advancing the future of humankind.

"We should also question pure science as such. Science has now triumphed over the idea of the unknown. We lull ourselves to believe that scientific miracles can rescue us from our fate. Science has decreed that it, in and of itself, is a good. That it is immune from ethical debate. Art is thrown into the debate of today—is art obscene or not, is it this or that. But no one asks if a particular science or experiment is obscene or not, because science has achieved a value in and of itself. We are reaching for the stars—when we are in fact digging our own graves. We need to bring science back under the scrutiny of ethics.

"We need to question fundamentally, the written word of some of our foremost thinkers, and ask, 'Does he really know what he is talking about?' 'Is it worthwhile to study John Locke? Does he say anything that makes any sense?' I can't see why anybody would tell anyone to study Machiavelli. We need to question whom we are going to look at for the models of the future. And I suggest to you, look at the words of Red Jacket, the Seneca orator. Look at the writings of Luther Standing Bear, the Sioux environmentalist. Look at the teachings of the Great Law of Peace, the Iroquois constitution. Look there, and you will find a lot, almost a textbook on how to run a planet, something that is sorely needed today. And something that I hope that educators of this city can dedicate themselves to achieving."

ABOUT THE AUTHOR

Hans Koning was born Hans Koningsberger in Amsterdam, Holland. He was in high school when the Germans invaded Holland; he escaped, to become one of the youngest sergeants in the British army during World War II.

After the war he ended up in the United States, arriving by freighter from Singapore, and ever since this country has been his home. Koning studied history but is by profession a novelist. Some of his best-known novels are *The Affair, A Walk with Love and Death, The Petersburg-Cannes Express, Death of a Schoolboy,* and *The Kleber Flight.* Several have been made into motion pictures. His forthcoming new novel is called *To the North Pole.*

Koning's nonfiction are political books, among them *Love and Hate in China, A New Yorker in Egypt, Nineteen Sixty-Eight,* and the autobiographical *The Almost World.* His *Columbus: His Enterprise* became "a basic document in the (1992) Quincentennial debate" and is now used in many schools and colleges. *The Conquest of America* is in a sense its sequel, carrying that story to the present day.